P9-CPZ-302

CULTURE SMART!
KAZAKHSTAN

Dina Zhansagimova

·K·U·P·E·R·A·R·D·

ISBN 978 1 85733 681 8
This book is also available as an e-book: eISBN 978 1 85733 682 5

British Library Cataloguing in Publication Data
A CIP catalogue entry for this book is available from the British Library

First published in Great Britain
by Kuperard, an imprint of Bravo Ltd
59 Hutton Grove, London N12 8DS
Tel: +44 (0) 20 8446 2440   Fax: +44 (0) 20 8446 2441
www.culturesmart.co.uk
Inquiries: sales@kuperard.co.uk

Series Editor Geoffrey Chesler
Design Bobby Birchall

Printed in Turkey

About the Author

DINA ZHANSAGIMOVA is a Kazakh journalist living in Almaty. After graduating in economics from the Kazakh State University, and gaining an M.B.A., she became a reporter covering news and current affairs for Kazakh television companies. She then joined the UN Development Program to work on social development projects in Kazakhstan, traveling to some of the most remote regions of the country. In 2003 she was invited to London by the BBC World Service to broadcast news programs in Kazakh. Later she moved to the BBC World Service Trust, the BBC's international development charity, where she ran a number of media projects in Eurasia, before eventually returning to Almaty.

The Culture Smart! series is continuing to expand.
For further information and latest titles visit
www.culturesmart.co.uk

The publishers would like to thank **CultureSmart!**Consulting for its help in researching and developing the concept for this series.

CultureSmart!Consulting creates tailor-made seminars and consultancy programs to meet a wide range of corporate, public-sector, and individual needs. Whether delivering courses on multicultural team building in the USA, preparing Chinese engineers for a posting in Europe, training call-center staff in India, or raising the awareness of police forces to the needs of diverse ethnic communities, it provides essential, practical, and powerful skills worldwide to an increasingly international workforce.

For details, visit www.culturesmartconsulting.com

CultureSmart!Consulting and **CultureSmart!** guides have both contributed to and featured regularly in the weekly travel program "Fast Track" on BBC World TV.

contents

contents

Map of Kazakhstan

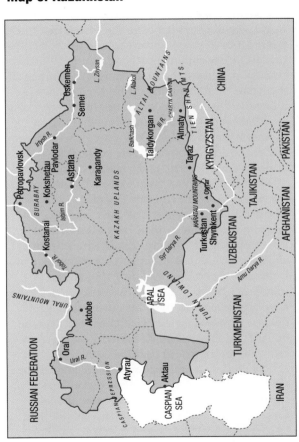

introduction

Kazakhstan, one of the largest countries in the world, was long hidden from the West—first under Russian tsarist rule and then behind the Soviet Iron Curtain. After gaining independence in 1991 the country continued to remain unnoticed among all the "stans" of Central Asia; now, twenty years on, it has emerged as a modern state with far-reaching ambitions. Free-market reforms and rising oil exports have made Kazakhstan the richest country in Central Asia. It has a vibrant economy, a stable business environment, and a friendly social scene.

The first thing that takes visitors by surprise is the sheer size of the country. For many of those who are reading this book on the inward flight, much of the journey will be over Kazakh land. Seen from the sky, the grasslands are a seemingly endless expanse, but although they may look a little featureless and dull to you they are a source of immense pride to the Kazakhs: these are lands they have kept against all the odds during their grim history. If people on the plane cheer and applaud on landing, they will be Kazakhs, rejoicing at the return to their beloved country.

The modern Kazakh people emerged after the rise and fall of a succession of medieval Turkic states, before being absorbed into the Russian Empire. They were self-reliant pastoral nomads, open hearted, generous, and tolerant, with laws of hospitality that put guests above all. These characteristics have survived to this day, so don't be put off by the serious faces that you will see in the street—these are just the masks that people grew accustomed to wearing to survive the hardships of the Soviet era. Once you get to know the local people, their genuine warmth, kindness, and loyalty will soon become evident.

There are many contrasts and extremes in Kazakhstan, and you may not like everyone and everything you see. You may find some of the apparent contradictions bewildering—not least, Asians speaking Russian, who follow a mixture of Muslim, Soviet, and earlier pagan traditions. This book sets out to introduce you to this complex, unknown nation. It guides you through its history, traditions, and social values so that you will be able to identify the signs of its Soviet totalitarian heritage, of Russian cultural influence, and of the Asian mentality with its deep respect for power and hierarchy. It tells you about the Kazakhs at work, at home, at leisure, and in the street; it describes how they celebrate their holidays, and what they eat and drink.

A review of Kazakhstan's dynamic business culture and economy shows that honesty and straight dealing are paramount when conducting business with local partners. Foreigners find it very pleasing to work and live in a country that is truly open and receptive to outside influences. All that is needed is a little patience and tact, and you will be rewarded many times over.

Kazakhstanga khosh keldingiz!
Welcome to Kazakhstan!

Key Facts

Country Name	Republic of Kazakhstan	
Capital	Astana	Second-largest city after Almaty
Main Cities	Almaty, Shymkent, Taraz, Aktau, Atyrau, Oral, Kostanai, Aktobe, Petropavl, Karagandy, Pavlodar, Semei, Oskemen, Kyzylorda, Taldykorgan	
Population	16 million (2009 census). 2013 estimates suggest nearly 17 million	Population density is low.
Area	1 million sq. miles (2.7 million sq. km)	Ninth-biggest country in the world
Ethnic Makeup	Kazakhs 63%, Russians 24%, others 13%	Others include Uzbeks, Ukrainians, Uighurs, Tatars, Belarusians, Germans, Koreans.
Border Countries	Russia, China, Uzbekistan, Kyrgyzstan, Turkmenistan	The country also borders the Caspian Sea, which is landlocked.
Climate	Acutely continental: dry, hot summers, very cold winters, and low precipitation. Milder in the south	Best times to visit are April–June and September–October.

Government	Presidential republic. Legislature is bicameral. Government is appointed by the President.	President is elected every five years by popular vote. Constitution allows for two consecutive presidential terms.
Literacy	99%	Kazakhstanis are entitled to free secondary education.
Languages	Kazakh and Russian	60% fluent in Kazakh; 85% fluent in Russian
Religion	Islam (70%) and Russian Orthodox Christianity (26%)	
Age Structure	Under 18, 26.4%; 18¬63, 63.6%; over 63, 10%	18–63 is the working age in Kazakhstan for women and men.
Unemployment	Just over 5%	
GDP per capita	11,400 USD (2011)	
Currency	Kazakh Tenge (KZT)	1 US Dollar equals around 150 KZT (2013)
Electricity	220 volts, 50 Hz	Two-prong plugs
Video/TV	PAL/SECAM	NTSC not supported
Internet Domain	.kz	
Telephone	Kazakhstan country code is +7 Astana code is 717 Almaty code is 727	To call out dial 8, then 10, and country code.
Time Zone	GMT +6	

chapter one

LAND & PEOPLE

GEOGRAPHY

Kazakhstan is a vast area of land in the heart of Eurasia, stretching nearly two thousand miles (3,000 km) from west to east, with a south–north range of more than a thousand miles (1,600 km). This huge territory is chiefly flat, covered in grass and shrubs, and is usually referred to as the Kazakh Steppe—a word of Russian derivation that can be defined as "terrain between forest and desert." Much of the Kazakh Steppe is semi-desert, and it gradually turns into desert farther south. The country is bordered by Russia's Ural Mountains in the northwest and a string of mighty mountain ranges along the south and east. The highest peak, Mount Khan Tengri ("Ruler of the Sky"), reaches nearly 23,000 feet (7,010 m). To the west lies the Caspian Sea, the largest lake on Earth, and the source of 90 percent of the world's caviar.

As many visitors to Kazakhstan can confirm, the size of the country really does matter, and not just from the traveling point of view. It is central to understanding the history of this place and its people. Endless grassland reaching the skyline, without a soul to be seen for many miles, is the essence of everything Kazakh. The territory is a staggering 1 million square miles (2.7 million sq. km)—about the size of Western

Europe—with a mere sixteen million inhabitants (2009 census), most of whom live in the larger cities. Away from the towns it is not unusual to drive for hours without meeting anyone. This is especially true for the least-populated central and southwestern areas of the country.

Kazakhstan is not as monotonous as it may sound, however. In fact, the country features an exceptional variety of landscapes that often contrast with one another. The steppe itself, primarily in the center of the country, can take you by surprise with its many fresh and saltwater lakes, which attract a great variety of waterfowl, and hilly areas that reach up to 4,900 feet (1500 m) in height. Southern Kazakhstan, which was once crossed by an important branch of the Silk Road, boasts the well-watered and forested Karatau Mountains (Black Mountains), an area rich in plant life and home to many rare birds.

In the north the steppe suddenly turns into a delightful and diverse region full of rivers, lakes, hills, and forests. These are some of the most photographed places in the country, famous among vacationers from

other regions and neighboring Russia. However, the most stunning views are to be found in and around the high Tien Shan, the mountain range in the southeast, and the Altai Mountains in the northeast. These two huge massifs are the main attraction—apart from the Caspian oil and gas industry—for most visitors who come to Kazakhstan.

The largest cities in Kazakhstan are Almaty in the southeast (the busiest and most developed in infrastructure), the entrepreneurial and trading city of Shymkent in the south, and the industrial town of Karaganda in central Kazakhstan. No less important are the new showcase capital of Astana in the north and Atyrau in the west—home to a large expatriate community working in the oil sector.

CLIMATE

Apart from its size, another distinctive feature of Kazakhstan is its distance from the sea in all directions: it is as landlocked as it is possible to be. The country's only coastlines lie on closed seas—the Caspian and the Aral—which are, in fact, classified as

"THE KAZAKH SWITZERLAND"

The most beautiful mountainous spots are naively nicknamed "the Kazakh Switzerland" by the locals. This stems from a sense of pride at the scarce and precious beauties that nature has given this otherwise plain land. A legend from Burabay, in Kazakhstan's north, reflects this. It tells how, when God created the Earth and its people, He began distributing mountains, seas, lakes, rivers, and fertile farmland among the different peoples. Everyone was happy except for the Kazakhs, who got nothing but endless, naked steppe. The steppe people asked the Creator to show them some mercy: can a whole nation survive in a land of bare steppe and desert? God looked inside his bag for the few treasures left, and threw all the remaining mountains, forests, streams, and lakes into the middle of the steppe. It turned out that those remnants were the best of all he had given—and that is how the most beautiful spot in the world was created. Burabay, its people say, is matched in beauty only by Switzerland.

lakes. This distance from the sea means that the country's climate is generally described as acutely continental, with hot, dry summers, very cold winters, and low precipitation. In the north the summer temperatures average 68°F (20°C) and winter temperatures average -4°F (-20°C). Extremes are not unusual: 104°F (40°C) in summer, and winter temperatures of -40°F (-40°C) are far from rare, especially in the central steppe and in the northeast. The ground is covered by snow for nearly six months, from late October to early April. Winds, including the occasional *buran*—the strong snowy wind from the northeast—are typical.

In the south the climate is milder, with less contrast, though summers are hot. In Almaty, the average temperature in July and August is 79°F (26°C), and by Kazakhstan standards the winters here are not as harsh as in the north, though temperatures occasionally fall to -4°F (-20°C). However, the high humidity levels typical of the area of Almaty, sheltered by the Tien Shan range, ensure that you feel the cold down to your bones. Sensitivity toward both the humidity and the outside temperature are different for local people and western travelers, so it is not always helpful to assume that what the natives are wearing is an indication of the temperature.

There are some winter hazards common to the larger towns and cities that you should be aware of. One is ice on the sidewalks—broken bones and sprained ankles are not unusual, even for ice-savvy locals. A second is that icicles fall from multistory apartment blocks; injuries from these are rare, but they can potentially kill. A third hazard is the marble floors in some new buildings, which can be extremely slippery when wet.

Further south, in the region bordering Uzbekistan, winters are much milder, with temperatures averaging 30°F (-1°C).

THE PEOPLE

Historically this land was populated by a Turkic people called the Kazakhs, meaning, in their language, free warriors or wanderers. They now comprise 63 percent of the country's population of more than sixteen million. The remainder is a mixture of nationalities that migrated or were forced to move to Kazakhstan as the price of coexistence with Russia's tsarist and Soviet regimes. The country's Slavic population is dominated by Russians (24 percent of the total population, or about 3.8 million people) and includes Ukrainians (330,000 people), Belarusians (70,000), and Poles (34,000). Other major groups include ethnic Uzbeks (nearly half a million), Uighurs (225,000), Tatars (around 200,000), Germans (nearly 180,000), and Koreans (more than 100,000). Turks (Meskhetian), Kurds, Greeks, Jews, Gypsies, and some of the North and South Caucasus ethnic groups are less distinguishable yet have long been part of Kazakhstan's history.

There is no formal or clear division of territories populated by one ethnic group or another, though southern parts are dominated by Turkic and Muslim groups (Kazakhs, Uzbeks, Uighurs, Chinese Muslim Dungans, Turks, and others) while the northern areas are largely settled by Slavic and German peoples. Culturally, however, there is no great distinction between the communities, due to the long shared history and common usage of the Russian language. In towns and cities the division is even less noticeable. Kazakhs are truly proud of the fact that since the breakup of the Soviet Union in 1991 there has been no noteworthy tension between the various nationality groups as in other parts of Central Asia. Some give credit to the traditional Kazakh values of tolerance and respect, and some to President Nazarbayev's success in restraining any outbreaks of nationalism.

Economically, Kazakhstanis are considered to be far better off than their Central Asian neighbors. Officially in 2010 there were just over a million people (6.5 percent of the total population) living below the minimum subsistence level. This figure was nearly five times lower than that for 2000. Government reforms of pensions and social welfare provision have succeeded in their attempt to address poverty in a comprehensive way. The official 2010 unemployment rate was 5.8 percent, half that of 2000.

These figures, however, do not reflect the disparity among social groups or the contrast between rural and urban life. In 2010 the top 10 percent had official incomes that were nearly six times greater than the bottom 10 percent. The actual gap is believed to be much greater. As in the other parts of the former Soviet Union, "the rich" are a relatively new class that emerged in the 1990s. Most are businessmen, who hugely benefited from early market reforms and privatization, and senior civil servants with power and connections to large business.

The poorest groups are to be found in the countryside, where nearly half of Kazakhstan's population lives. The rural poverty level is three times higher than that in towns and cities. You don't need to travel far into the heart of Kazakhstan's steppe to realize that the rural economy is in a submarginal state. The outskirts of the country's brand new capital, Astana, are a grim reminder of the fact that Kazakhstan is still a country in transition, with a long way to go to achieve prosperity for all its people.

If, however, you are in the heart of one of the bigger cities, like Almaty, Astana, or Atyrau, you are most likely to encounter the well-educated and fairly prosperous middle class. These are people who have

adapted well to recent economic changes. The
younger they are, the more likely they are to be
progressive thinkers, free from the Soviet legacy,
and eager to get the most out of their lives.

The Kazakhs
The Kazakhs are the dominant ethnic group in the
country, but this wasn't always the case. Russia's
imperial and then Soviet policy led to sharp falls in
the Kazakh population during the nineteenth and
early twentieth centuries. Many fled from new
administrative changes and taxes imposed by the
tsarist government, and many more died or were
killed during the years of starvation and genocide of
the 1930s Stalinist era. By 1939 there were fewer than
2.5 million Kazakhs left in the country. The picture
changed after the breakup of the Soviet Union in 1991,
when many of Kazakhstan's Russians, Germans, and
other ethnic groups that had either been forcibly
settled in the country or had immigrated willingly in
recent centuries chose to move back to their historic
lands, while ethnic Kazakh communities living
abroad started to settle back in Kazakhstan.

Kazakhs are generally perceived by fellow and
neighboring nations as a very tolerant and open
people who value two main things above all: peace,
and their guests. Nomadic in the past, the Kazakhs
have kept their friendliness and tradition of care
toward travelers and newcomers, whether these
visitors feel overwhelmed by the grasslands or just
alone and awkward in an unfamiliar place.

In appearance, Kazakhs have Asian features,
but there are distinctions between the browner
southerners and the fairer-skinned northerly type;
manners, language, and general conduct, however,

really show the difference. Northern Kazakhs tend to regard the southerners as unintellectual and boastful, but respect their business sense; Southerners regard most of their northerly compatriots as being too slow in making decisions and generally boring. The most arrogant of all may be the inhabitants of Almaty—Kazakh or of any other nationality—who regard themselves as much more sophisticated because of the city's historic capital status.

As mentioned above, many Kazakh families that had fled the country in the early twentieth century are returning to settle there. Since independence, nearly half a million ethnic Kazakhs have been repatriated to various parts of Kazakhstan. They are called *oralmans* (returnees), and they form a new and unique group in modern Kazakh society. They managed to preserve the Kazakh language and customs while living abroad, and are also bringing back aspects of other cultures. While much has been done to support them in their resettlement, their economic and social integration remains a significant challenge. They are one of the most vulnerable groups living in the country, lacking the means and the skills to prosper in their new environment. Some have successfully integrated, but many have chosen to return to the regions from which they originally came. It is sad that local

Kazakhs who had previously demonstrated remarkable tolerance toward newcomers from various backgrounds in the earlier periods of history are showing a less welcoming attitude toward those returning.

The Russians

Russians are the second-largest ethnic group living in the country. They dominated the population during the years of the Soviet Union, but millions migrated to Russia in fear of economic depression and discrimination after the Union's breakup in 1991. Their fears did not materialize, and some of those who left in the early days of independence have since returned, but their status as citizens of independent Kazakhstan has changed.

Even though Russians still represent nearly a quarter of the country's population, their current representation in the government is minimal in comparison to the earlier Soviet period, when Russians were not just an ethnic majority but were also the political and social elite. At independence the Kazakh language became the official "state" language, and although Russian was given special status, remaining the main language used in the public sector, the change was hard for the non-Kazakh population, especially those in middle age. During the Soviet era Russian was introduced as the official language, and the general policy was that knowing Kazakh was not necessary. As a result, many Kazakh families, especially those in the bigger cities, lost their knowledge of their language. Official use of Kazakh is still quite limited, and learning it is not yet the norm.

The younger generation of Russians has adapted well to living in the newly created state. Russians nowadays are the bedrock of the country's urban middle class, owning small and medium-sized businesses in the manufacturing, trade, transport, communication, IT, and service sectors. However, wealthier Russian families try to send their children to study at Russian or Western European universities, preparing the ground for their smooth relocation in the future.

On an individual level there is a strongly sympathetic attitude, across all levels of society, toward Russians, who are regarded as honest, hardworking, and conscientious. Intermarriage between Russians and other nationality groups is still not common, but lifelong friendships are often made.

The Rest
A small percentage of the population are neither Kazakh nor Russian. Most of these people were settled under a number of forced Soviet migration campaigns before and following the outbreak of the Second World War. Then, in the 1950s, many more immigrated willingly as part of the Virgin Lands campaign to cultivate cereals in the steppe. Some ethnic communities, such as the Uzbeks and the Dungans, had settled in Kazakhstan long before the establishment of the Soviet Union in 1917 for reasons of trade, business, and agriculture.

Most of these long-settled immigrants live in the southeast and south, the most fertile areas of the country, in distinct communities with their own subcultures and traditions. The main sources of income are agriculture—especially the growing of fruit and vegetables—and trade. The younger generation, notably Koreans and Azeris, are increasingly working in the bigger cities, in business, the financial sector, and banking.

THE LANGUAGES

Kazakhstan is a bilingual country. The dominant language used across all strata of society, especially in towns and cities, is still Russian, in which, according to the 2009 census, 85 percent of the population are fluent. Russian has special status as a language that can be used alongside Kazakh in government and public institutions.

Kazakh is the state or national language, and is promoted as a priority language to be used by government institutions and in Parliament. Its actual use by politicians is limited, however, due to the large number of Russian-speaking civil servants who do not know it well enough. It is widely used at an informal level, but less so during official meetings or in correspondence. However, it is the dominant language among the rural population, and about 60 percent of Kazakhstanis are fluent in Kazakh.

There is growing criticism over the constitutional status of Russian from some parts of the Kazakh community, who see it as the main obstacle to the development of Kazakh as the first language in the country. On the other hand, there are fears that stripping Russian of its official status may lead to another wave of emigration by Russian and other Slavic communities.

English is understood by about 15 percent of the population, with fewer than 8 percent conversing and writing fluently. Even on the streets of the biggest cities in Kazakhstan a visitor cannot expect to be understood in English.

A BRIEF HISTORY

Modern-day Kazakhs trace their direct racial ancestry to Turkic nomadic tribes who migrated to this region from what is now Mongolia and northern China. The early Turks, however, were not the first nomads to come to the vast steppe lands now known as Kazakhstan. Between 500 and 200 BCE, the land was home to the early nomadic warrior culture of the Saka (Scythian) tribes, who had migrated from the Black Sea coast to the foothills of the Altai Mountains, replacing earlier Stone and Bronze Age settlers.

The Turks

The earliest Turkic-speaking peoples to arrive from the East were the Usuns, the Kangui, the Alans, and the Huns. They settled the Kazakh steppe lands from around 200 BCE to 500 CE. Around 550 CE the first feudal state, the Turkic Khaganate (empire), presided over by a *khagan*, or emperor, emerged. Later in the seventh or eighth centuries this empire was superseded by another Turkic tribe, the Tyurgesh. These were strong empires that prospered from the fabled Silk Road, a trading corridor that linked Europe to China and played a significant role in the commercial, cultural, and political development of the Central Asian steppes.

Despite its strengths, the region was unable to withstand attacks from the Arabs, who began their conquest of Central Asia under the banner of Islam

in the mid-eighth century. They attacked the
Tyurgesh Empire, eventually causing the Khaganate
to collapse. Gradually Islam replaced Tengrism,
Buddhism, and other religions that had hitherto
been widespread. The Arab conquest also brought
the Arabic script, which was to replace the Turkic
alphabet previously in use.

Later the Arab Caliphate weakened and in 766 a
new Khaganate was established in the far south of
Kazakhstan by another nomadic Turkic tribe, the
Karluks. In 940 their state was taken under the
control of yet another semi-nomadic people, the
Karakhanid tribe. The Karakhanids had by and large
adopted Islam, and many took up a more settled
way of life, cultivating fruit, vegetables, and cereals.

In the twelfth century the Khaganate fell to a wave
of attacks from the east, and the Muslim Karakhanid
tribe were displaced by the Karakitae, a Buddhist
people from the territory that is now Mongolia.
They created a new Central Asian state known as
the Karakitay Empire.

Meanwhile the Oghuz Turkic tribes were settling
in the steppes around the Aral Sea in Western

THE GOLDEN AGE OF THE KARAKHANIDS

This was a period of overall stability and growth that benefited the development of southern cities such as Taraz and Yassy. (Around the fifteenth century Yassy was renamed as Turkestan, the name used by Russians to label the entire region.) It was also during the Karakhanid period that famous thinkers and writers lived and worked—men like the great philosopher Al-Farabi, who is known for his detailed study of philosophy, astronomy, music, and mathematics. The well-known scholar of Turkic philology Mahmud Kashgari also lived at this time. He wrote a three-volume dictionary of Turkic dialects that to this day is an important source on the history of Turkic folklore and literature. Another epic dating from this time is *Kutadgu Bilig* ("Blessed knowledge"). Written by the famous poet-philosopher Jusup Balasaguni, this book is regarded as one of the first literary monuments to the aesthetic thoughts of the Turkic people. The Sufi poet Hodja Ahmet Jassawi lived during the twelfth century in what today is southern Kazakhstan. His collection of poetic thoughts *Divan-i Hikmet* ("The Book of Wisdom") is known throughout the Muslim world.

Kazakhstan. Their state was soon absorbed by yet another powerful nomadic tribe, the Kypchak, known in the West as the Cumans. Through the next few centuries more nomadic tribes—the Kidans, Naimans, and Kerei—left their traces on the region's culture and history.

The Mongol Empire

In 1218 the fearsome army of the Mongol leader Genghis Khan attacked Zhetisu, the area of southeast Kazakhstan known as "the Land of Seven Rivers" (Semirechye, in Russian), between the Tien Shan mountains and Balkhash Lake. The Mongol warriors then moved south to Bokhara in present-day Uzbekistan, Afghanistan, and India, and west as far as Hungary and Poland. Along the Syr Darya River alone more than thirty cities were completely destroyed.

These captured territories became part of the vast Mongol Empire, and were in due course shared among Genghis Khan's four sons. The northern and western parts of modern Kazakhstan went to the eldest son, Juchi, and became known as the Golden Horde. (The word "horde," derived from the Turkic *ordu*, means a tribal army encampment.) The second son, Chagatai, took Zhetisu, southwestern regions of present-day Kazakhstan, and the territories of Uzbekistan and Afghanistan. The share of the third son, Ogedei, included China and territories further east. The youngest son, Tolui, inherited the Mongol heartland.

The Golden Horde played the most important role in the later formation of the Kazakh homeland as a unified nation state. After years of war, prosperity came to the territory. Trade blossomed and many towns were rebuilt. Open intertribal war ceased. Due to their similar languages and culture the tribes coexisted peacefully, paving the way for the formation of tribal confederations, or *zhuzes*, the core of the Kazakh nation, that survive to this day.

Genghis Khan's grandson, Batu, expanded the Golden Horde's territory. He campaigned as far as Crimea on the Black Sea coast, and his domains eventually stretched from Irtysh in the east to Khorezm in the southwest, and to the Lower Volga in the west. His capital was Sarai-Batu, the present-day Russian town of Saratov.

This period came to an end in the late fourteenth century. Weakened by infighting and divisions among Genghiz Khan's descendants, the Mongol Empire began to disintegrate. Emir Timur, or Tamerlane (c.1336–1405), who was associated by marriage with the house of Chagatai, became ruler of Mawarannahr (Transoxiana) and Central Asia, and carried out a number of devastating campaigns against the Golden Horde. A devout Muslim, Tamerlane built his own empire, with Samarkand as its capital. This included the far south of Kazakhstan.

The Golden Horde split into a number of smaller states, the largest of which were the Ak (White) Horde and the Kok (Blue) Horde. The Ak Horde was a significant political force, rich in territory and manpower, that strengthened its position under Urus Khan (*khan,* ruler) in the 1360s and '70s. However, internal power struggles and the external threat posed by Tamerlane's state led to the Ak Horde's eventual collapse and the appearance in its place of a number of smaller states, including the Abulkhair Khanate. Its ruler, Abulkhair Khan (1412–68), was descended from Batu Khan's brother, Shaiban. He extended his original territories to encompass the whole of modern-day north and northwest Kazakhstan. These events coincided with the rise of Mogulistan in southeast Kazakhstan, in what remained of the Kok Horde.

The Kazakh Khanate (1456–1847)

Abulkhair Khan was a zealous Muslim. Under his rule, the tribes and their leaders were required to observe Islamic laws and regulations. This and other policies made him unpopular among some of the *sultans* (members of the nobility), such as Zhanibek and Kerei, who in the mid-fifteenth century broke away from the Khanate for good, taking with them a number of tribes. These tribes were the first to be called Kazakhs.

In 1465–66, following the gradual concentration in Zhetisu of all those discontented with the policy of Abulkhair's state, Zhanibek and Kerei proclaimed the Kazakh Khanate. Its influence grew rapidly, and flourished vigorously under Kasym Khan, an accomplished military leader and wise politician who was also known as "the gatherer-in of Kazakh lands." Under his rule the Khanate ended up stretching from the Ural range to the Syr Darya River, and from the Caspian Sea to Zhetisu.

The state was divided into three regions—Senior, Middle and Junior—occupied by the main tribal confederations. The Senior Zhuz took the area between the Syr Darya and Zhetisu, the Middle Zhuz occupied central and northern Kazakhstan, and the Junior Zhuz settled on the banks of Aral Sea and in the Mangyshlak Peninsula, near the Caspian Sea.

The Kazakh–Zhungar Wars (1723–30)

In the seventeenth century the Khanate started suffering from severe internal instability. A continuing struggle for power in the Khanate and strong social polarization weakened the state in the face of new external threats. The main challenge was posed by the Zhungars, a Lamaist–Buddhist tribe in western China that had formed the Zhungarian Empire in 1635. In the late seventeenth century they started a grueling war for the pasturelands of Zhetisu and north Kazakhstan.

At first their increasing attacks led to a consolidation of forces within Kazakh society. Kazakh-wide gatherings (*kurultay*) took place on a regular basis and a united defense force was formed, but by 1723 the Zhungars had become a formidable military force that eventually crushed the Kazakh army. Many Kazakhs died on the battlefield, but many more succumbed to the famine and illness that afflicted the steppes as a result of the war. It was one of the darkest periods in Kazakh history, known as *Ak Taban Shubyryndy* ("the Years of Great Disaster").

A later wave of resistance was led by *batyrs* (warlords) from the tribal aristocracy of the time. Their efforts brought a short-lived victory to the Kazakhs. The Zhungars came back in 1741, however, when Kazakh society was once again torn apart by tribal rivalry and power struggles.

Russian Colonization

Feeling vulnerable in the face of the militarily stronger and more numerous Zhungars, in 1734 the Junior Zhuz aristocracy under Abulkhair Khan (not to be confused with the fifteenth-century Abulkhair) concluded an agreement with Russia to accept its "protection" against external threats. The agreement left Abulkhair all powerful in matters other than external relations. In return for Russia's protection, he promised to deploy his own forces to ensure the security of Russia's trade caravans across his territory.

Later the other two *zhuzes* signed similar pacts with Russia to deny Abulkhair the possibility of seeking Russian support in any internal political struggle. However, they had underestimated the power these treaties gave to Russia. The documents inadvertently paved the way for Russia's initially peaceful colonization of Kazakh territories. Russia chose to interpret the agreement as an annexation pact, and started expansion. Landless Russian peasants were sent to settle and farm the land; pasturelands were confiscated from locals; and a strict tax system was introduced. By the middle of the nineteenth century most Kazakh lands were under Russia's direct control.

Naturally, revolts followed right across the steppe, but Russia's grip was already too tight to be broken. More than a quarter of the population is believed to have died during the uprisings and famines that repeatedly occurred as a result of Russia's claim to

Kazakh territories. Many people, hoping to preserve their traditional way of life, fled to neighboring states.

Kazakh Autonomy

In the summer of 1916 a powerful revolt broke out. Russia was preoccupied by the First World War, which exposed all the weaknesses of the Tsarist regime. The war caused poverty and hunger throughout the Russian Empire. In June 1916 an imperial decree was issued, and Kazakhs were conscripted into forced labor groups while their cattle and property were confiscated for military use. This appeared to be the last straw.

The uprising that became known as "The Great Revolt" swept across Central Asia. It was harshly suppressed at first, but erupted once more after the February Revolution of 1917. The formation of the first Kazakh political party, Alash, raised the stakes for the national liberation movement with its demand for full Kazakh independence. The first Kazakh Congress, held in October 1917, appointed a provisional autonomous people's council of Kazakhs and gave it the task of drafting a democratic constitution with a system of government presided over by a president.

Soviet Rule

If the February Revolution gave the colonized nations of the Russian Empire some hope of self-determination and independence, their hopes were dashed when the Bolsheviks, a wing of the Marxist Social Democratic Party led by Vladimir Lenin, came to power in November. Civil war started. By the spring of 1918, Soviet power had been established in Kazakhstan through a combination of voluntary acceptance of the new principles and force of arms. On August 26, 1920, the Kazakh Autonomous Soviet Socialist Republic was created as part of the Union of Soviet Socialist Republics (USSR). Initially it comprised both Kazakh and Kyrgyz territories. In 1936 this was split into separate Kazakh and Kyrgyz republics, each of which was given enhanced status as union republics.

The leaders of the Alash party and their supporters were executed, and other intellectuals sent to labor camps or exiled. Kazakhs were prohibited from following their traditional way of life. Stalin's wider "collectivization" program forced the previously nomadic population to settle in designated areas and to hand over their livestock to collective farms. Those opposing the policy were harshly punished, deported, or killed. Yet the hardest times were still ahead. Almost two million people died of starvation when famine swept the country as a result of collectivization, which also caused the disease and death of expropriated animals. Another million Kazakhs fled to neighboring China and

Mongolia, with some moving further to Afghanistan, Iran, and Turkey. The Kazakhs lost nearly half of their population.

Regarded as suitably empty and remote, Kazakhstan began to be used as a place of exile for those considered real or potential threats to the Soviet system. In the years preceding the Second World War entire peoples were deported *en masse* from various areas of the USSR: Poles from Western Ukraine and Belarus, Volga Germans, Crimean Tatars, Kalmyks, Chechens, Ingush, Balkars, Karachai, and Meskhetians from Crimea and the northern Caucasus. Bulgarians, Greeks, and Armenians were among those forcibly relocated from the Black Sea coastal region. After the German army invaded Soviet territory these peoples were accused of collaborating with the German occupation forces. Needless to say, many of those deported starved or froze to death, either during their hard and long journeys to Kazakhstan or after arrival.

Furthermore, prison and labor camps were built in central and north Kazakhstan—vast and sparsely inhabited regions with no roads or sources of food, but rich in natural resources. Inmates were put to hard physical work, providing cheap labor for entire economic sectors of the Soviet Union, especially to help the war effort. In the mid-1950s, when Stalinism began to be denounced, virtually all the labor camps were closed down and the surviving inmates freed, yet many stayed on in Kazakhstan.

In the years that followed, more Russians, Ukrainians, and Belarusians arrived to take advantage of the new opportunities brought about by the extraction of coal, iron, uranium, oil, and other resources, and formed new industrial towns.

Another 800,000 people migrated under the so-called Virgin Lands Campaign initiated by Moscow in the mid-1950s. Vast territories of steppe land in north Kazakhstan were irrigated and plowed to grow wheat. Water was taken from the Amu Darya (Oxus) and Syr Darya (Jaxartes) Rivers through newly built canals. The environmental downsides of the project were greatly underestimated. Only in the late 1980s did the catastrophic effects of the scheme on soil and landscape become apparent.

This was by no means the only environmental disaster of the period. The Semey *oblast* (region) in the northeast was the site of a forty-year experiment—exploding nuclear weapons in the atmosphere, at ground level, and underground. The Aral Sea, formerly one of the largest inland lakes on Earth, nearly died as most of its waters had drained away in another large-scale experiment that aimed to turn desert land into cotton and rice fields. And finally, the issue of the safe disposal of waste residue from decades of mining uranium, copper, and coal all across the industrial areas of the country has yet to be addressed.

Traditional Kazakh culture and language have also experienced their greatest challenges in the nation's recent history. Becoming a minority in their own country, the Kazakhs had little opportunity to pursue their traditional way of life, while in the new Soviet world they were treated as second-class citizens without a history of their own and without a need to preserve their language. This doesn't mean that the Kazakhs lost themselves as a nation, but the Soviet experience has had a substantial impact on what the nation is today.

Yet at the time, under the years of Soviet-style socialism, Kazakhstan made impressive leaps forward in the development of its economy, in its general and higher education, and in science. The country was transformed from a feudal state with a vast area of pasture for nomadic livestock breeders into a region with a large-scale industrial complex, a developed agriculture, and a livestock breeding system. By 1991—the moment of declaration of independence from the Union—Kazakhstan had become a modern, secular state with a strong extractive and industrial base, a developed economy, a well-equipped army, and good scientific potential.

Independence

In December 1986 a massive riot took place in
Alma-Ata (now Almaty), the capital city at the time.
Thousands of students protested the appointment
of Gennady Kolbin—an official of Russian descent
who had never lived or worked in Kazakhstan—as
leader of the country's Communist Party. This had
nothing directly to do with Kazakhstan's declaration
of independence later in 1991, but it was indicative
of a political shift that was spreading across the
Soviet Union at that time.

The protest started in Alma-Ata on December
17, following the issue of a decree on Kolbin's
appointment the previous day. It spread to other
big towns, and lasted for several days. Protesters
were harshly suppressed. According to officials only
two people died as a result of clashes between the
police and protesters, and around a hundred people
were detained, with some being sent to labor
camps. However, the details surrounding the
"December Events," as they became known,
remain locked in Moscow archives, giving rise to
speculation about the actual numbers of dead
and persecuted.

Following the protests in Almaty, similar unrest
broke out in other parts of the Soviet Union. In the
wake of a deepening economic and political crisis
the central leadership in Moscow was seriously
weakened, and unable to retain its control across
the country's fifteen republics. Finally, in February
1990, the Communist Party made a number of
constitutional changes to allow for a more liberal
political structure. These changes paved the way for
a process sometimes described as a "sovereignty
parade," when local parliaments at republic level

one after another started declaring their states sovereign within the Soviet Union.

Kazakhstan's sovereignty was declared on October 25, 1990. The dissolution of the USSR, however, had already begun. The dissolution was complete by December 1991, despite attempts to preserve some form of union of sovereign states and even a *coup d'état* attempt by former KGB officials in Moscow.

Kazakhstan was the last to proclaim its political independence. Nursultan Nazarbayev, who had headed the republic's Communist leadership since the 1980s, was elected president of the independent republic in January 1991. He adopted the Law on

Independence on December 16, 1991, the anniversary of the Zheltoksan events of 1986 that had triggered Kazakhstan's emergence as an independent nation.

Kazakhstan Today

The transition period following independence was not easy. Liberalization of the economic system started with the abolition of price controls in January 1992. This resulted in enormous inflation. In November 1993 a national currency, the tenge, was introduced, bringing the value of the Soviet rouble, in use at the time, to next to nothing. Industries came to a virtual standstill without ways to export their products, and workers were laid off with no means of survival. Savings vanished overnight. Remembering these times still brings a chill to Kazakh citizens today. The countryside was under threat of starvation, and a great influx of people into the towns and cities took crime levels to their highest ever.

Yet the latter years of this bumpy decade brought a wide variety of opportunities for those with natural business sense, and a spirit of entrepreneurship started to develop. Most found themselves in small trade and business, while some managed to create great fortunes from the early privatization of state enterprises. Foreign investment started to flow into the energy sector, and gradually brought the country's economy to life. Local production of food, light industrial goods, and agriculture grew. The country eventually became self-supporting in food, which was considered a big step.

Twenty years on from independence, Kazakhstan has become a politically stable and economically prosperous country. It has built a reputation as the Central Asian pacesetter, thanks to its economic reforms and wise foreign policy. The country's leadership is carefully trying to balance relations with bigger powers, such as the United States, Russia, China, and the European Union, each of which has a stake in the country's economy.

However, bigger challenges lie ahead. The 2007 economic crisis showed that Kazakhstan's economic prosperity is extremely vulnerable because of its dependence on raw materials. Diversifying the economy, fighting massive-scale corruption, addressing the disparity in wealth among the population, and moving toward a more liberal political system are only some of the tasks ahead. It is not clear whether Kazakhstan will be able to resolve all these issues, as they require fundamental changes to its internal policy. All that can be said at present is that the nation is well aware of them.

GOVERNMENT AND POLITICS

The 1995 Constitution provides for a democratic, secular state and a presidential system of rule. The president is head of state. He appoints the government with the approval of the lower house of parliament, the Majilis, and has influence on the composition of the parliament's upper house, the Senate. In case of a vote of no confidence against the government, he can dissolve the Majilis. The president has the right to present bills and decrees and decides whether or not to hold referenda. In addition, he is the commander-in-chief of the armed forces, has the right to appoint and dismiss their leadership, and can proclaim a state of emergency in the country.

The president is elected by popular vote for a five-year term. The last elections were held in 2011 and

were won by Nursultan Nazarbayev, who has been in power and practically unchallenged since independence from the Soviet Union in 1991. In May 2007, in accordance with the principles of the Organization for the Security and Co-operation in Europe (OSCE), the Constitution was amended to allow only two terms for a president. It also reduced the presidential term from seven to five years. Furthermore, these amendments allowed for greater government accountability to parliament. The changes are meant to initiate a gradual transition from a "presidential democracy" to a "presidential–parliamentary democracy." The same amendments, however, made an exception for the current president, who can run for office any number of times and potentially stay in office indefinitely. In 2010, MPs granted Nursultan Nazarbayev the lifelong title of "leader of the nation."

State governance is divided among the executive, legislative, and judicial branches. Parliament, we have seen, consists of the Senate (the upper house) and the Majilis (the lower house). Most senators are elected by assemblies of local representatives, while fifteen are appointed by the president. The Majilis, which functions as the main legislative body, has 107 MPs, with ninety-eight elected through party lists and nine provided by the Assembly of the People of Kazakhstan, a council of ethnic minorities. In the elections to the Majilis of 2012, Nursultan Nazarbayev's Nur Otan party won the majority of seats (eighty-three seats out of the ninety-eight elected through party lists). The elections were yet again criticized by international observers, but were locally regarded as historical, as two other parties gained a foothold in parliament for the first time. The true value of parliament, however, remains questionable, as it is not regarded as an influential political institution, having no authority to appoint the government or to have a final say in setting the state budget.

The excessive concentration of power and authority in the hands of the president and his administration is said to be justified by the necessity to undertake swift economic reforms and preserve interethnic stability. This approach seems to be popular among the bulk of Kazakhstan's population, despite criticism from Nursultan Nazarbayev's political opponents—such as former senior civil servants and some businessmen, the most outspoken of whom have left the country to seek asylum in Western Europe after facing persecution in Kazakhstan. Press freedom is guaranteed by the Constitution, but private and opposition media are kept on a tight leash by the government's use of unpopular media laws.

Administratively, the country is divided into fourteen administrative districts (*oblasts*). Almaty and Astana, the former and current capital cities, have their own administrative status and do not belong to any *oblast*. Each *oblast* is headed by a governor (*akim*) appointed by the president, and is subdivided into smaller districts (*rayons*). The *rayons* are governed by *rayon akims* and their offices (*akimats*). Since 2006 the majority of *rayon akims* have been elected by local representatives (*maslikhats*). Village *akims* are elected directly by the people.

THE ECONOMY

Kazakhstan is the largest economy in Central Asia and the second-largest in the former Soviet Union, after Russia. Its economy demonstrated high growth rates over the last decade, reaching an average of 10 percent real GDP growth. This was interrupted by the global financial crisis in 2009, when growth

plummeted to 1.2 percent. However, as a result of commodity prices strengthening on world markets and extensive governmental anti-crisis measures, Kazakhstan's economy was relatively quick to recover, and grew by 7.3 percent in 2010.

The country's economic growth is largely driven by extractive industries, which account for almost 20 percent of GDP. Kazakhstan produces up to 1.5 million barrels of oil daily, placing it eighteenth on the list of the world's largest oil producers. According to the US Energy Information Administration, full development of its major oilfields could make Kazakhstan one of the world's top five oil producers within the next decade. Although a significant oil exporter, Kazakhstan experiences regional and seasonal oil product shortages due to its low refining capacity and the difference between domestic and international oil prices. Apart from oil and gas, Kazakhstan contains Central Asia's largest recoverable coal reserves, and is the second-largest coal producer in the former Soviet Union, after Russia. It is also endowed with rich reserves of chromite, lead, zinc, and uranium, as well as bauxite, copper, gold, iron ore, and manganese.

Despite its rich mineral resources, national manufacturing comprises only 11 percent of GDP and is characterized by low levels of productivity, lack of innovation, and outdated technology. Other significant sectors of the economy are wholesale and retail trade (13 percent of GDP), transportation (8 percent), construction (7.7 percent), and agriculture (4.5 percent). The construction sector's vulnerability was demonstrated in 2008–09, when a shortage of capital investment from abroad led to a credit crunch and stagnation in construction.

While acknowledging the risk of dependence on oil and extractive industries, Kazakhstan aspires to become a modern, diversified economy with a high value-added and high-tech component. To this end it has embarked upon an ambitious diversification program that aims to boost the country's potential with industrial innovation. By 2015 Kazakhstan aspires to join the fifty most competitive nations expanding non-raw-material exports and increasing the contribution of manufacturing to GDP. However, despite these well-defined objectives, progress lags behind the targets and independent economists are skeptical about the program, citing such factors as high levels of corruption and nepotism, and governmental interference into market forces.

Integration into the global economy is also seen as an important driver of economic development. Kazakhstan is at the final stage of negotiations to join the World Trade Organization (WTO). In addition, on January 1, 2010, together with Russia and Belarus, Kazakhstan formed a trilateral Customs Union and is now firmly moving toward a Eurasian Common Economic Space that will enable free movement of goods, services, capital, and labor among the three countries. The planned accession to the WTO and formation of the Customs Union have been subjects of heated debate among local producers and businesses, who continuously express concern about the low competitiveness of local manufacturing in both global and regional markets.

THE ENVIRONMENT

Most of Kazakhstan's environmental problems are a legacy of the former Soviet system. Its territory suffered from extensive military testing and space launches, for example. The northeastern region of Semey was most severely despoiled, being the place where the Semipalatinsk nuclear test site operated for forty years. Nowadays the central part of Kazakhstan, home to the world's largest space launch facility, Baikonur, is under constant environmental threat from falling fragments of rockets and highly toxic fuel.

Another inherited disaster is the massive erosion of the soil and the impoverishment of natural landscapes that resulted from the forcibly imposed Virgin Lands campaign of the 1950s. Under the campaign the Soviet government undertook to cultivate wheat on a massive scale by irrigating the steppes of northern and central Kazakhstan. After fifty years of over-intensive cultivation, the living steppe has been transformed into dead semi-desert. Some sources estimate that the country has lost 1.2 billion tons of topsoil. Furthermore, the excessive agricultural development across the country resulted in universal degradation of soil. More than 60 percent of the country's territory is now exposed to desertification.

The Aral Sea is yet another distressing reminder of the manmade disasters of the Soviet period. Once the world's fourth-largest inland lake, with a uniquely rich ecosystem, the Aral has now broken up into a number of lakes, having lost 80–90 percent of its water as a result of poorly planned irrigation systems. The southern part, bordering Uzbekistan, is considered to be a lost cause, but the northeast corner (Little Aral) has started to fill up with water again due to the efforts of the Kazakhstan authorities and support from

international aid agencies. There are serious fears, however, that the tragedy could be repeated at the lake of Balkhash, which is rich in fish and other wildlife. Excessive industrial use of water from the Ili River, which runs into Balkhash, and emissions from the Balkhash metallurgical complex are the main reasons for anxiety.

As a whole, the rapid expansion of extracting and manufacturing industries has been most detrimental to Kazakhstan's environment. Among the most harmful are lead-zinc production in Oskemen in the northeast, lead-phosphate production in Shymkent and phosphate production in Taraz, both in the south, and the chrome enterprises in Aktobe in the northwest.

A new environmental threat now causing concern is oil pollution in the Caspian Sea, where extensive exploration and extracting activities have affected both the temperature of the seawater and the humidity of the atmosphere, and have led to the extinction of rare fish and other live organisms. The destructive effect of oil pollution is especially evident among the birds that live on these waters, and stocks of sturgeon are falling.

Despite numerous environmental programs developed by the large extractive companies and the government under the pressure of international organizations and civil society, it seems that environmental protection and conservation are still not top priorities. Public ignorance, underestimated risks, indifference, and the public bodies' inability to influence state policies and business practices all contribute to the lack of progress.

chapter two

VALUES & ATTITUDES

Kazakhs are proud of their national identity, and most of their customs are rooted in their pre-Russian nomadic history and traditions. But more than two hundred and fifty years of Russian presence and Soviet rule have influenced them, while the growing prosperity of recent years has Westernized many people to some degree.

In the countryside traditional Kazakh values prevail, though they are mixed with Soviet-style submission to and faith in authority. The southern and western parts of the country are especially conservative in their attitudes, due to the greater influence of Islam. In the northern and eastern parts the ambience is more Soviet, and the general atmosphere is that of a Russian territory. At the same time, the bigger cities, such as Almaty and Astana, seem to epitomize a mixture of all the past influences, with their inhabitants trying to look Western and bourgeois, despite often lacking the credentials for either.

TRADITIONAL KAZAKH VALUES

A modern Kazakh might feel ashamed of the nation's linguistic assimilation under the Soviet system, but there is one thing of which he or she is surely proud,

and that is the feeling of *Kazakshylyk*, or "Kazakhness," shaped by a system of values preserved from the people's nomadic past. These values have kept Kazakhs together over hundreds of years and are still central to their identity.

Seven Fathers
In Kazakh culture, knowledge of one's ancestry is paramount. It is the essence of Kazakhness. You know who you are, and you know that you are Kazakh if you are able to recount at least seven generations of your paternal ancestors, then your clan, your tribe, and finally your tribal confederation, or *zhuz*. In the past this was how people in Kazakhstan would define themselves.

A male ancestor who is seven generations away from a senior living relative gives a name to a sub-clan (*el*, in Kazakh). The *el* is a part of a wider clan (*ru*). Clans are united into a tribe (*taypa*), and tribes are grouped into a tribal confederation (*zhuz*). There are three major tribal confederations: the Senior, Middle, and Junior Zhuz. Each had its own territory, where there were semi-fixed pastoral routes for every tribe and their clans.

THE STRUCTURE OF TRADITIONAL KAZAKH SOCIETY

The Senior (*Uly*) Zhuz united the tribes of the Alban, Dulat, Suan, Ysty, Oshakty, Shapyrashty, Zhalayr, Kangly (Sergeli), Sary Uisyn, and Shangyshkyly. Historically it occupied the fertile regions in the southeast of the country, stretching as far as Uzbekistan's Tashkent region. The Middle (*Orta*) Zhuz inhabited the vast areas of central, north, and northeastern Kazakhstan and included the tribes of the Argyn, Nayman, Kypchak, Kongyrat, Uak, and Kerei. The Junior (*Kishi*) Zhuz was settled along the Syr Darya River, on the banks of the Aral Sea, the Caspian Depression, and in some southern parts of what is now Russia. The tribes of the Baiuly, Alimuly, and Zhetiru belonged to it.

Prior to Russian colonization each tribe had a *soultan*, while each *zhuz* was led by a *khan* elected from among *soultans*. Descended from Genghiz Khan's eldest son, Juchi, *soultans* were recognized as members of the nobility, and were called Tore. They did not belong to a *zhuz*—like Kozhas and Saids, who were originally Sufi missionaries spreading the word of Islam among the Kazakh tribes. Tore, Kozhas, and Saids formed a local aristocracy not only in Kazakhstan but also across other parts of Central Asia.

Virtually all pastoral societies are built around patrilineal kinship groups. Such social organization is necessitated by the nature of nomadic pastoralism, the rules of which are strictly dictated by the environment. The minimal unit of Kazakh society was a community of two to five families, closely related through their male heads, which looked after shared stock. During the winter season these small communities lived autonomously, separated from each other by the grassland on which their animals fed. In spring, wider clan communities joined up in their designated summer pastures in numbers dictated by the size of their stock. In other words, life was organized around the needs of the herds and within kinship groups.

Kazakh folk tradition considers that all clans and tribes have a common forefather named Alash. "We are children of Alash" is an expression that shows how Kazakhs feel united as one nation. Nowadays, with no real nomads left and kinship having no practical value, knowledge of one's ancestry and genealogy still makes sense to people as a means of defining their national identity. Researching complex genealogical trees called *shezhire* and determining kinship ties among the various clans has acquired a new purpose today, with Kazakhs trying to establish who they are after almost a century of Soviet rule.

Family Relationships and Hierarchy
The smalll unit of two to five families mentioned above formed a basic stockbreeding community called an *aul* ("village" is the closest meaning). These units were typically formed of a man and his married sons, with their families. Newly married couples either lived with the husband's parents under a shared roof but within a separate dwelling, or "raised their own *shangyrak*" (the roof of a traditional Eurasian nomadic home, called a *kiyiuz ui*, a *yurt*, or movable

felt house) due to the need for more living space, or once they had enough stock of their own. The youngest (or only) son and his family do not follow this rule, and stay with his parents for good. Girls are expected to leave the house when they marry. There is a saying that a daughter is merely a guest in her parents' house.

The tradition of male relatives staying so close to each other was called *ata-balasy* ("the rule of grandfather and sons"), and the principle remains common today. You can raise your own *shangyrak* by living in a separate house or apartment, but you must pay regard to (in order of importance) your grandparents, parents, uncles, aunts, brothers, sisters, cousins, nephews, and nieces, your wife, and your children. On marriage, a man's family forms a ready-made family for his wife, and most of the couple's free time is spent together at the father's house, under *kara shangyrak*, the main roof.

Such close relationships within a wide family are reflected in the language as well. For example, the word *aga* is equally used to address elder brothers, cousins, and uncles—in fact any senior male relative. Similarly, senior female relatives are all called *apa*. There are special names for younger siblings, nephews, and nieces, but these differ depending on whether the person addressing them is male or female.

There is a strict hierarchy within a family based on an age seniority principle called *ulken–kishi* (senior–junior), which also applies to social relations within the wider society. In family life it means many things. First, the elderly are held in great esteem and are never abandoned. Second, the senior members of the family are expected to take care of those who are younger and to share responsibility for their education and career. The young must follow the advice of their seniors and make themselves available for the wider family's day-to-day needs. Children over the age of six are considered old enough to bear their share of family responsibilities, helping about the house and showing respect toward their elders.

Ulken-Kishi
A widely known Kazakh proverb says: "If a senior person comes to your house, serve them food; if a younger person comes, find them work."

However, the extent to which such traditional relationships are preserved varies. Urban families are less strict in following traditions, often having more Westernized views. Women of the younger generation prefer to live separately from their husband's parents and to build a more independent family of their own. Even rural communities are more flexible these days, with most of the young departing to cities for study or work. In the country's south and west, however, the traditional way of family life is cherished and preserved, having become mixed with Islamic attitudes toward gender roles.

SPIRITUAL VALUES
Pre-Islamic Turkic beliefs and practices remain an important element of spirituality in Kazakhstan. Much to the disappointment of foreign Islamic missionaries and *imams* (priests), most Kazakhs still

value ancestral cults centered on saints and places deemed holy by early nomads. These beliefs are remnants of the ancient Turkic beliefs of Tengrism and shamanism followed by local tribes before the spread of Islam.

Tengrism can be classified as a monotheistic natural religion. The cults of Sky (Tengri), Earth, Water, Fire, and Fertility are central to the belief. Tengrism still has a strong following among Mongols, a few Altai communities in Russia, and, to a lesser extent, in Kyrgyzstan. There is very little information on the evolution of Tengrism and its earlier predecessors, such as shamanism. Yet, many modern-day Kazakh values and traditions have their roots in those pagan beliefs.

For example, there is still great reverence toward the spirits of ancestors (*aruah*). When Kazakhs pass a burial ground they will raise their hands and pull them toward the face—a purely nomadic gesture, rather than Islamic—and say a short prayer in Arabic or a simple "Amen." Another tradition is that of making *shelpek* (fried flat bread) every Friday, a holy day in Islam, in the belief that the ancestral spirits will appreciate the smell and the memory.

The spirits of revered individuals and tribal forefathers are especially cherished. In southern Kazakhstan the burial sites of Father Baidabek (Baidabek Ata) and Mother Domalak (Domalak Ana) are considered to be holy, as they are believed to be the parents of a son who was the forefather of the three major Senior Zhuz tribes—the Alban, Suan and Dulat. Burial sites and mausoleums are often the main attractions that tourists encounter in the wide steppes of Kazakhstan.

Certain natural places, such as caves, strangely shaped rocks, and lone trees, are also held in great regard, especially by women, who will approach them to pray to the spirits and ask to be cured from illness or infertility—which many believe can be caused by the anger of ancestral spirits. To find a cure, the person may go to a *baksy* (shaman), a person regarded as blessed by Allah and as having access to, and influence in, the world of spirits.

THE SOVIET LEGACY

Seventy years of Communism had a huge impact on the way Kazakhstanis think and act today. Many still feel a little nostalgic for the past, especially those who were already on the doorstep of their pension at the time of the Union's collapse. There were also many people— such as farmers, doctors, school and university teachers, and members of the armed forces—who simply found it hard to adapt to a new, less regulated life. Having expected to retire on a decent pension, they were suddenly left with virtually nothing.

But if romanticizing the past is confined to one particular group in society, there are a number of values and behavioral attitudes left over from Soviet times that are universal. Years of political repression under Stalin left the deepest mark in people's minds. The fear of being detained, interrogated, and sent to prison or a labor camp for the slightest political criticism hasn't loosened its grip over the wider public even three generations later, much to the advantage of the current authorities. Furthermore, the absolute supremacy of one single ideology and one single party—the Communist party—during all those years has led to political apathy and sluggishness on the part of the country's citizens. Public demonstrations are extremely rare and are harshly suppressed, which doesn't help to speed up the liberalization process.

At the same time, most people still subscribe to an over-paternalistic view of the state, the government, and, especially, the figure of the president, who is seen as (and indeed is) the only person who can resolve deadlocks in the country's economic, political, social, and spiritual life. It is interesting that authoritarian presidential rule is not regarded as a mechanism for the repression of individual rights but rather as a means of enabling those rights.

Rough manners in public transport, on the street, and in public places are still the norm, as they were across the former USSR due to the terrible hardships, hunger, and mass imprisonments of the past. Prison and labor camp manners spread and flourished across society following the amnesty of those people imprisoned during Stalin's rule. Constant shortages of consumer goods often meant standing in long— very long—lines, which people deeply resented. As a result, former Soviet citizens, their children, and, it turns out, even their grandchildren, cannot bear the thought of standing in line. They will do anything to cheat their way into the line—behavior that makes the experience even worse.

There is very blurred understanding of the terms "privacy" and "private life." Several decades of communal life, shared property, and being similar in all aspects of living have made these words alien to local ears. To many people it is not considered impolite to ask questions about your salary, savings, and private life, yet a foreigner asking the same questions risks being taken for a spy—another little phobia inherited from Soviet times.

But of course life is not all phobias and fears. Despite its extremes, Communism produced highly literate societies with low levels of income inequality. Kazakhstan was no exception. Literacy levels greatly increased, with a positive effect on attitudes to education, hygiene, health, sports, and other aspects of life. Employment of women was both boosted and celebrated, leading to increased acceptance of a role for women in the workplace. Equal opportunities and access to education meant greater social mobility among classes, reducing class barriers all round. Children across all strata of society are still raised in the genuine belief that if you have brains, guts, and enough resilience you ought to succeed in life.

RELIGION

Islam is the dominant religion in the country. Traditionally, Kazakhs, Uighurs, Uzbeks, Dungans, Azeris, and some of the North Caucasus nationalities define themselves as Muslims, while the Slavic population of Russian or Ukrainian origin, for example, is predominantly Orthodox Christian. There are also many independent communities of believers. The feeling in the air is secular, however, although the number of churches, synagogues, and especially mosques is growing fast.

Historically, the Kazakhs never saw themselves as a religious nation. There was always a degree of resistance among nomads to accepting the norms and rulings of Islamic Sharia laws. Even today Islam is strongest in the south, close to Uzbekistan, among historically sedentary communities, where Islam gained a strong foothold as early as the eighth century, during the rule of the Karakhanids.

In the rest of the country, Islam fused with elements of Tengrism and earlier shamanistic beliefs. Islamic traditions were observed during major community and family events, but were not part of everyday life. Then the Soviet era came, and its policy of aggressive atheism left no trace of any religion whatsoever.

After independence there was a general increase  of interest in religion, including Islam, and in time foreign missionaries came to Kazakhstan in great numbers, preparing the ground for the formation of various religious organizations and sects. Access to Islamic education opened up through funding from religious schools in countries such as Turkey and Egypt. The sight of bearded men and of women wearing the *hijab* (headscarf) and long, loose dresses has become common in cities and countryside alike.

At first the official take on the issue was rather liberal. But then a number of armed incidents involving religious groups led to a sharp tightening of legislation, with the government imposing strict controls over certain religious organizations and activities, despite warnings and objections from religious communities and human rights groups. In 2011 the government banned prayer rooms in state buildings and required all missionaries to register with the authorities every year.

POSITION AND POWER

Kazakh society gives special importance to official position and power. Thus the civil service attracts a great number of young graduates, all of whom aspire to become top-ranking officials. Having a family member who has achieved the authority to manage others is the ambition of many households. The nation's love for obtaining elevated, powerful, and profitable posts is vividly displayed at wedding banquets, when the families of the bride and the groom try to outdo one another in ranks and titles.

WOMEN

In the workplace Kazakhstan is one of the most equal societies. Although there are proportionately more women in lower-paid jobs, discrimination on the basis of gender is not evident. It becomes more apparent, however, in the home and family. Women who work a full day outside the home are expected to cook, clean, and care for the children inside it as well. In rural areas, and especially in the south and the west, where the influence of Islam is noticeably stronger, women are generally confined to the role of mother, wife, and daughter-in-law.

In the rest of Kazakhstan, women have always enjoyed more freedom, due to a lesser dependence on Islamic laws. It is fair to say that even in the southern areas of the country the cultural conditioning of  women has been less rigid than elsewhere in Central Asia. Women were never required to wear veils or long robes, for example, and girls were given access to basic education if the family could afford it. Then, during the Soviet Union, emancipation was encouraged as part of the wider Communist ideology of social equality. Having said that, ultimate dominance in society evidently belongs to men. This can be seen mainly in family life and, especially, in politics.

As elsewhere in Central Asia, women constitute a vulnerable social group. Cases of domestic violence with female victims are not at all rare. Furthermore, poverty in rural areas leads to the rise of prostitution in the bigger cities, with many women becoming entrapped by international human trafficking gangs. Sadly, the issue fails to capture public attention, and is regarded as only a minor problem. Considering that women dominate the media industry, it is interesting that this is so.

On a personal level, most women are extremely feminine in attitude and behavior. In the Kazakh language the word *inabatty* reflects the perfect combination of the characteristics desirable for a woman: she should be modest, humble, utterly respectful (especially to men and the elderly), gentle, sensitive, empathizing, generous, and caring.

This doesn't mean, of course, that every woman embodies all these attributes, though the culture of a traditional Kazakh upbringing encourages parents to raise their daughters in this spirit so that they will understand their future roles as mothers, wives, and daughters-in-law. These roles, however, will differ somewhat according to where one lives, with a woman in the countryside usually being more dependent on her husband and his family than if she lived in a city.

ATTITUDES TOWARD EDUCATION

Kazakhstan has a literacy rate of almost 100 percent. Education is one of the things for which the old Soviet system should be given credit. Schooling was good, covered almost all of the population, and was free. The earlier, pre-Soviet schools were private, fee-paying establishments that catered to only a miniscule portion of the population; poorer families had few opportunities to give their children any sort of education, with the rare exception being lessons at local mosque-based schools teaching basic Arabic.

It was probably the scarcity of well-educated men in that period that made education seem as valuable as religion to the masses. It is also possible that stripping people of their religious beliefs during the Soviet period led to the formation of this other belief—a belief in education. Indeed, doing well at school in Soviet times usually meant that a child was guaranteed a prosperous future, consisting of higher education and a stable job in the chosen field, with good career prospects.

Nowadays everyone is still entitled to free secondary education, but the quality has fallen since independence due to a shortage of textbooks and other materials, underfunding, especially in rural schools, and very low rates of pay for teachers. The best schools are by and large in the bigger cities, and are privately funded. Fortunately the strong belief in education has been preserved—teachers, parents, and pupils are all very serious about learning.

The consequence of this is an incredibly high demand for university education. No one wants to be a factory worker, for instance; young people aspire to become corporate managers, governors, or inspectors of some sort. Thus giving a higher education to your offspring is a matter of honor for every family. The brighter children often have a chance to receive sponsorship or a loan from the government. Less fortunate ones are financed by their families, who can often barely afford it. Yet this enthusiasm has to some extent backfired, as it has led to the creation of hundreds of private institutions that have dubious entry standards and provide low levels of education.

Those who can afford it attend universities abroad. The most talented young people compete for annual presidential educational stipends called Bolashak ("the future"), which guarantee the winners full sponsorship for masters' and PhD degrees at international universities.

Sadly, the country's scientific base, which was highly developed in Soviet times, has all but disappeared. The Academy of Sciences was closed, with only a few of its institutes preserved and reorganized. Those aspiring young people graduating from secondary schools with the highest marks—most of whom are very talented and eager to work in science—have very few in-country prospects for developing their careers.

ATTITUDES TOWARD WORK

Kazakhstan is a country with rather modern views about workplace relationships. Yet attitudes toward work vary from sector to sector, from generation to generation, and from one geographical area to another. There are also some local peculiarities of which a foreign employer or a colleague should be aware.

Kazakhstanis, even as varied as they are, are perceived in the region to be highly educated and hardworking, and on the whole you will find people to be punctual and willing to work.

The work culture in the private sector, which offers better financial incentives than the state, is the closest you can find to that in the Western world. There is a competitive environment, and the matter of human resources is taken seriously, so there are better choices of personnel, better motivation, better communication, and so on. People are generally prepared to work overtime if a task requires it, and absenteeism is rare.

Working in Kazakhstan's public services—such as transport, social services, utilities, education, health care, fire control, and waste disposal—has its own specificities. Public sector employees typically earn much less than those in the private sector, and recruitment standards are lower. Hiring relatives and friends is not uncommon. Above all, the work culture in the public sector has changed little since the old Soviet days, despite some reforms. Bureaucratic and unhelpful staff are the norm, and petty bribery is commonplace.

Geographically there are slight differences as well. Southerners are widely perceived as people who act and learn fast at work and have entrepreneurial spirit. They are more traditional when it comes to values, however, and thus respect clear hierarchy and strong leadership in the workplace. Northerners have a reputation for being slower in pace and more stubborn in general, but they are direct and open in their dealings, with strong principles of delivering honest hard work. Naturally, the larger cities have more educated and professionally developed workforces, with younger people often being able to speak English and Kazakh along with Russian.

chapter three

CUSTOMS &
TRADITIONS

All in all, Kazakhs form a traditional society that cherishes its old customs. Most of the widely used rituals pertain to the three main stages of a person's life: birth, family formation, and death. The rituals vary slightly from one region of Kazakhstan to another, but generally have similar meanings and goals. All are the result of fusion between early pre-Islamic Turkic beliefs and more recently acquired Muslim traditions.

The influence of tradition changed considerably during the Soviet era, when many customs were forcibly suppressed. New celebrations based on Communist ideology were imposed, and most of today's formal national holidays can be traced back to this period. After independence yet another set of celebrations became part of Kazakhstani life, with some Soviet holidays having been transformed and a few older Kazakh and Islamic traditions revived.

BIRTH AND INFANCY

Most Kazakh traditions are linked to the arrival of a newborn baby—an event full of old superstitions and beliefs. Nowadays these have mainly symbolic meaning, yet they are widely followed. Pregnant women, for example, try to adhere to a traditional set of rules that include prohibitions on eating certain types of food (camel, rabbit, and fish), cutting hair, going out at night alone, and taking part in burial ceremonies. A woman in labor lets her hair fall loose and removes all jewelry—a rule still strictly enforced in maternity hospitals. If the labor takes too long female relatives gather and boil meat, in the belief that a baby should be born sooner than meat is cooked. This is called *zharys kazan*, or "competing with a cauldron."

After the baby is born a celebration among relatives is organized, called Shildekhana, which is sometimes delayed until after the symbolic forty-day threshold. During these forty days the baby is not expected to be widely seen, and remains nameless. Traditionally it was believed that a newborn infant is attached to the underworld and can easily die. At morning prayer on the fortieth day the child is finally named by the eldest person in the family. He either reads aloud from the Koran or says a simple *Bismillah* ("In the name of God," in Arabic), and whispers the name three times into the child's ear.

This is followed by another ceremony, in which the child is washed in a bowl with forty spoonfuls of water purified by silver coins and jewelry, and his or her hair and nails are cut. The silver is divided among the women taking part in the ritual, and a special blessing by the elderly is given to the child before all those gathered.

When a child makes his or her first attempts to walk, another old ritual, *tusau kesu* ("cutting the nets") is observed. A specially prepared intertwined black and white thread is tied to the child's ankles, and a guest chosen by the parents then cuts these bonds, saying, "Fly like the wind; be a man!" The child is then encouraged to take a few steps over a piece of white material symbolizing a clean and open "road of life."

In the case of boys another important ritual is observed at the age of five or seven, when the time for circumcision has come. This could be the only Muslim tradition that was not abandoned during Soviet times.

Each of these occasions is usually celebrated with a lavish *toi* (banquet), an obligatory accompaniment to most rituals observed by modern Kazakhs. This usually entails sacrificing an animal—usually a sheep—and asking for a *bata*, or blessing, from the elderly. The blessing is given in Kazakh, and is accompanied by a recitation of Koranic verses in Arabic if someone able to perform it is present.

WEDDINGS

There is a strict rule in Kazakh society that marriage partnerships must be made outside one's own lineage, going back for seven generations. Those with a common paternal ancestor fewer than seven generations away are considered as brother and sister. The rule is less strict on the mother's side, however, and does not apply to other ethnic groups.

Provided that this "rule of seven fathers" is not broken, people today are free to make their own choice of spouse. Thanks to years of Communist rule, class differences in modern Kazakh society are not great enough to be an insuperable obstacle. In pre-Soviet times, however, the choice was made solely by the groom's parents long before he reached marriageable age.

Having made the decision to marry, the couple follows the traditional process, which starts with the "asking" stage, or *kuda tusu*. Matchmakers (*zhaushy*) go to the prospective bride's house to obtain general agreement and to set a date for the official visit of the groom's parents and relatives to settle the dowry (*kalym*), though nowadays this often has more symbolic value than anything else. If a substantial dowry is paid it is usually given to the newly married couple anyway. Then, on the agreed-upon date, the groom's family makes the official visit to the bride's family with the formal proposal of marriage. They come bearing the richest gifts they can afford, which usually include various  garments for the bride's relatives and a bag with expensive sweets, delicacies, and sometimes wine, if the family is not devoutly Muslim. Separate gifts are given to the bride and her mother. In the bride's case it must be gold earrings. For their part, the bride's side prepares lavish treats for the guests, entertaining them in the best possible way and often presenting similar gifts.

Finally, the wedding date is set and both sides discuss the couple's future life. It is usually the responsibility of the groom's side to provide the newly married couple with their living accommodation. If there is enough room the couple will simply join the groom's parents, following the *ata-balasy* rule, mentioned in Chapter 1. Otherwise the groom's side arranges to provide an apartment or house, which the bride's side will equip with furniture and essentials.

The wedding itself is usually in two stages. First, the bride's side gives a banquet, called *kyz uzatu*. The guests are by and large the bride's relatives, with a limited delegation from the groom's side. The purpose is for the bride's relatives to say farewell to her. Then she is taken to the groom's parents' house in the company of his female relatives. From that moment she is considered to be a married woman with a new family of her own. When she leaves her family she must not look back, under any circumstances, as this is regarded as a bad sign, a superstitious belief that she might return to her parents, which would be considered a matter of great shame. "The daughter who comes back is as bad as an enemy," says an old proverb.

The second and main stage is on the day the couple is officially registered as a married couple and blessed in a mosque by an *imam* (priest). In towns and cities these ceremonies are followed by a new type of ritual in which the bride and groom are driven around the city for several hours to have their pictures taken at various symbolic points. On this day the groom's family gives the wedding banquet (*uilenu toi*), which starts with one of the oldest Kazakh rituals, called *betashar*, the uncovering of the bride's face. The ritual starts with a song sung by a bard (*zhyrau*), who is familiar with the groom's family, the purpose being to introduce them to the bride. The bard mentions details of their characters and positions. As their names are recited the relatives step forward and offer gifts, or, more commonly, place money into a special bowl that is later presented to the bard. The bride bows every time she hears a name, as a sign of respect. At the end of the ceremony the bard removes the bride's veil and guests are invited to start the feast.

To spare their families all this lavish expenditure, some young couples just agree to run away, in a semblance of the old bride-kidnapping tradition, but this is not generally regarded as an honorable start to a marriage. In cities, parents may simply meet in a restaurant to agree on the wedding and other arrangements that satisfy both sides. Russian and Slavic families in general also have less strict wedding rituals, either adapting them or simply ignoring them altogether.

MOURNING AND REMEMBRANCE

Remembrance of the dead is held sacred, and the burial place of ancestors is regarded by every Kazakh as a homeland forever. The burial and mourning of a deceased family member is the most ritualized area of Kazakh traditions.

If a person's death is imminent, his close relatives should inform others, so that everyone has a chance to say farewell or ask forgiveness for past disagreements. This is called *aryzdasu*. The dying person tells the family how to distribute his property upon his death, requests a particular burial location, designates someone to prepare his body for its final rites, and gives instructions about the kind of tomb or memorial dome to construct.

The deceased person's body is kept for three days in a separate room, for in early times Turkic people believed that the soul of the deceased person would remain among the family for two days, departing for heaven on the third. This also gives relatives living in remote places the chance to come for the funeral. During these three days, the body is guarded by senior members of the family, or the closest ones, and a candle is lit at night. Relatives and friends come to express their condolences and offer help. The burial arrangements and all the logistics involved in welcoming the guests are taken care of by relatives of the deceased person. This is one occasion when a Kazakh feels grateful for the tradition of close kinship ties.

On the evening before the funeral, guests are invited for a special dinner, *konak asy* ("dinner for guests"), served by relatives at the home of the deceased. A sheep must be slaughtered on this day. On the next morning, after having been washed by three to five chosen male relatives, the body is wrapped in white cloth and a rug. A special memorial service, *zhanaza*, is performed by a *mullah* (Islamic priest), then the body is brought to the burial site. The grave is no more than chest deep and the vault must face Mecca. The grave is not filled in with earth, but is simply covered with planks or stones.

The burial is followed by a dinner for everyone gathered, with the proceedings opened and concluded by a *mullah*, who reads a prayer in Arabic. A similar remembrance dinner is served on the

SUPERSTITIONS

Kazakhs don't hide the fact that they are a superstitious nation. There is an old saying, "Kazakhs believe in signs, while signs go twisted and awry." Superstitions underlie many of the local cultural traditions stemming from early Turkic paganism. For example, you should never leave someone's house without at least tasting the host's food—even if you just stepped in for a few minutes to discuss business. If you arrived just as the family was starting to eat, you will be told that you are a truly good man and must share the meal. You should not turn down the invitation, as this might cause suffering in the home. On leaving you will be given a *sarkyt*, something from the host's table.

Various actions are said to bring bad luck. Never tread on the threshold, but always step over it with your right foot. Also, beware of greeting anyone across the threshold. Once inside the house you should not turn your, or anyone else's, shoes upside down (taking off shoes at someone's home is a must). If you see that a shoe is turned over immediately put it on your foot, or it may cause death.

Some other popular "don'ts," if ignored, can bring misfortune. Never fake a cry; don't wipe a table with paper; don't run in the direction of your or anyone else's home; don't sit on a threshold; don't put your hands on your waist; don't sleep during sunset, and don't start a journey on a Tuesday or on the ninth day of a month.

fortieth day of mourning, and another after exactly
a year. The latter marks the end of the mourning
period. A horse, or if necessary a less expensive
animal, is slaughtered for the special meals on the
day of the funeral and on each of the following
memorial occasions.

TRADITIONAL HORSEBACK GAMES

In the countryside, physical sporting contests are a
frequent accompaniment to many special occasions.
Given the significant value of the horse in the once
nomadic Kazakh society, the most popular of all are
racing and various horseback competitions.

Horse racing in Kazakh is called *baige*. It is a
rare treat much beloved by the public and is usually
organized by wealthy families as part of other
festivities, such as a wedding or a circumcision
celebration, or by local authorities to mark the
anniversary of some historical figure. The prize is
announced in advance: it might be a car, or a
substantial amount of money.

The most popular type of race covers distances
of about thirteen to nineteen miles (21 to 31 km), or
even longer. These races are called *alaman baige*. The
number of participating horses is flexible, since the
competition is usually held on the open steppe, but
they should be more than five years of age. Younger
horses have their own races, called *kunan baige*,
over various distances depending on their ages.

Another popular race is *kyz kuu* ("catch the girl").
Young men on horseback pursue a girl, also on
horseback, who gallops off just ahead of them. The
horseman who catches her and, on the gallop, kisses

her cheek (or, in another version, unties a scarf from her arm) wins the competition.

Known farther south in the region as *buzkashi,* there is another popular sporting competition that Kazakhs call *kokpar*. It is a sort of horseback rugby, where two teams of horsemen compete and wrestle to grab a headless goat carcass. The team that succeeds must then throw it across the opposing team's goal line.

PUBLIC HOLIDAYS

There are eleven official public holidays in Kazakhstan's current calendar. They are all state holidays, except for Independence Day, which is classified as a national holiday to stress its importance in Kazakhstan's history. All these days are marked red in the calendar and are official days off work.

New Year	January 1–2
Orthodox Christmas	January 7
Kurban Ait	Varies in accordance with the lunar calendar
International Women's Day	March 8
Nauryz	March 21, 22, 23
National Unity Day	May 1
Victory Day	May 9
Astana Day	July 6
Constitution Day	August 30
Day of the First President	December 1
Independence Day	December 16 and 17

New Year

Similar to other parts of the former Soviet Union, the favorite of all the festivities are the New Year celebrations, which last for two days. The tradition of welcoming and celebrating the New Year came into people's lives rather forcefully— as was often the case with the Soviet regime—in the late 1930s, but since it was the only holiday that people were allowed to take, it quickly settled into the Soviet nations' hearts and minds. The festival's attributes and decorations resemble those of a Catholic Christmas: a tree, the Russian version of Santa Claus (called Ded Moroz, or Ayaz Ata in Kazakh), gifts, and sweets. Fireworks are also a necessary part of the celebrations. New Year's Day is generally regarded as a time when families get together; after midnight the younger members usually go out to party till morning.

Orthodox Christmas

There are a large number of followers of Russian Orthodox Christianity in Kazakhstan, totalling nearly 25 percent of the population. Orthodox Christmas has been celebrated officially since 2005. It falls on January 7, according to the earlier Julian calendar in use in Russia until 1918.

Celebration of the Orthodox Christmas is fascinating to witness, and has a wonderful atmosphere. The main church service starts at midnight, with bells ringing, people carrying candles, priests chanting, choral music, and the fragrance of myrrh.

International Women's Day

Originally called International Working Women's Day, this is marked on March 8. Once a purely socialist event dedicated to the celebration of socialist women's political achievements, it was later transformed into a warm and much loved holiday resembling, as someone put it, "a combination of Valentine's Day and Mothers' Day." Everyone gives something to their mothers, grandmothers, aunts, and sisters, and women are overwhelmed with flowers and small gifts.

Nauryz

This initially Zoroastrian holiday has become a
widely celebrated festival in many countries of
central and western Asia. Among Kazakhs it has
become associated with early Turkic philosophy and
nomadic traditions. Forbidden during Soviet times,
Nauryz was reinstated in Kazakhstan after the USSR's
collapse. It has now become a festival at which old
Kazakh traditions and rituals are coming back to life,
giving the nation an opportunity to feel its cultural
identity. Once celebrated for a whole month,
nowadays Nauryz festivities last for three days,
March 21, 22 and 23, coinciding with the vernal
equinox. Yurts selling traditional food appear in
main squares and streets, along with tents selling
handicrafts, stages for traditional singers and dancers
to perform their arts, and plenty of loud music.

In homes festive Nauryz tables are laid with seven
different dishes. The most important of all is *Nauryz
kozhe* (soup). Each family has its own recipe, but the
general rule is to include seven ingredients: water,

meat, salt, oil, flour, grain, and fermented milk. These are to represent happiness, luck, wisdom, health, wealth, growth, and the protection of the sky, which, as we saw in an earlier chapter, has been considered sacred from the time of Tengrism.

Victory Day
Nearly a million Kazakhstanis died fighting in the Soviet army against Nazi Germany during the Second World War (also known as the Great Patriotic War in former Soviet lands). There is hardly a family without its sad personal history related to the war and without a relative who was lost in battle. Thus it is no surprise that this is one of the most cherished holidays in Kazakhstan, just as it is in many other former Soviet Union republics. Though veterans are fewer in number every year, and criticism mounts over the policy and tactics used by Soviet leaders of the time, this doesn't seem to change public attitudes toward the May 9 commemoration. (The surrender document was signed late in the evening on May 8, 1945, thus on May 9 by Moscow time.)

Astana Day (and Day of the First President)
These are the most controversial holidays in the calendar. Astana Day, on July 6, coincides with the president's birthday. It is a big, lavish party for the city, with lots of entertaining events, concerts, performances, art exhibitions, and parades—a party well worth joining. The celebrations are widely broadcast through several TV channels and radio stations across the country. Much of the controversy relates to the amount spent on organizing the event, which often includes exorbitant fees paid to foreign singers and celebrities.

Kurban Ait (Eid el-Adha)

This is one of the two religious holidays recognized officially in Kazakhstan, the other being Orthodox Christmas. Both were introduced not long after the breakup of the Soviet Union. The date of Kurban Ait (Festival of Sacrifice), or Kurban Bairam, as it is known in the wider Muslim world, change according to the lunar calendar. It is one of the most significant and most devoutly observed Muslim holidays. On the day a Muslim should sacrifice an animal and distribute two-thirds of the meat to the poor, with the rest going toward the holiday meal. One person can sacrifice a sheep, and a group of up to ten people can sacrifice one head of cattle. The animal should be young and without physical defects. The festival commemorates the sacrifice of a ram by Ibrahim (Abraham) in place of his son.

Independence Day

This is the only holiday in the country's calendar that is officially classified as "national" rather than "state," meaning that it has utmost importance in the nation's history. It is a celebration of the country's

independence from the Soviet Union that was declared on December 16, 1991. It is also a day to commemorate victims of the 1986 demonstrations known as the December Events (described in Chapter 1). Official events include award ceremonies to the nation's most outstanding artists, athletes, scientists, and others. There is no tradition of big family dinners, however, as people prefer to go out, gathering in the main squares for various performances and concerts. Two days—December 16 and 17—are official days off.

SUBBOTNIK

This is a Soviet tradition that is not massively popular, and yet it has survived to this day in some shape or form. *Subbotnik*—from the Russian word *subbota,* meaning Saturday—is a day of unpaid voluntary labor, usually on a Saturday. It is associated with post-winter cleaning such as sweeping streets, collecting garbage, and washing windows. People also plant trees and lawns. *Subbotniks* are usually organized by city authorities and supported by municipal companies and their workers. For private sector office workers this day simply means an opportunity to clean their desks. Some modern *subbotniks* can be charitable, raising money to support disabled or old people, orphanages, and children with HIV or cancer.

chapter four

MAKING FRIENDS

The Kazakhs, and Kazakhstanis in general, are very friendly and open. This might not be obvious when you walk on the streets, where people may seem a little serious and uninviting. On closer acquaintance, however, you will realize that interacting with locals is a pleasant experience, thanks to their natural warmth and desire to be helpful, which stems from a traditional culture of hospitality. Yet, turning your relationships into true and close friendships either takes a long time or requires a powerful shared experience that makes people feel close to one another. From a foreigner's perspective, knowledge of at least the Russian language is crucial; otherwise, the circle of your potential local friends will be very limited.

FRIENDSHIP

Friendship in Kazakhstan means a very close bond. It is thought to be real happiness when you have a close circle of friends, or at least one real friend among your acquaintances. Real friends are people with whom you enjoy spending time, but they are also people you can count on when you are in trouble—for example, to help you find a job, or a good doctor, or to lend you money. Attitudes toward friends and friendship may change depending on your age, stage of life, and gender.

Your local playground, school, and university are typical bonding places, where close friendships are built to last for years, and even for a lifetime. Parents who can afford to live in a good neighborhood and to choose well-respected schools do  so to ensure that their children are exposed to the best influences, which are also likely to last for many years. An inability to build close friendships at school is considered to be a misfortune. If such relationships aren't built at university, the person is regarded as odd and unsociable.

A close friendship is strongest early in adult life, when interests are shared and desires are common. Later, after marriage, close friendships may go through a serious trial due to a natural shift of focus to the spouse and small children. In an ideal scenario the relationship with a friend turns into a new form of friendship with a family, but some relationships are weakened and may eventually collapse. New friendships that are perhaps more compatible with a family-oriented lifestyle may be built at the workplace, but these rarely reach the same emotional attachment as older ones. Friendships with some sort of practical value for both sides are also made.

In Kazakhstan a woman and a man rarely choose each other as friends: women are friends with women, and men with men. Naturally, friendship means slightly different things to both. Women's friendship is often regarded as unreliable and fragile, but strong bonds forged between girls of school age often last a lifetime. For a Kazakhstani woman a friend is someone you can talk to for hours about your problems—even the most intimate ones. For men, that much talking is unusual, although occasional sharing of feelings certainly happens. Typically, male friends come together to play and watch football or hockey (the two most popular games in Kazakhstan), and to discuss the big news of the day, including sports, business, and so on. Inviting one another home is becoming less popular in cities unless someone wants to throw a welcome party in a new house or invite a friend who is visiting from another town or country. Friends typically meet at restaurants or cafés, or go out for a picnic.

Unlike in the West, people do not usually befriend their neighbors or meet through clubs. You simply maintain good terms with your neighbors, or chitchat with someone at the gym every day, without going further. Pushing these boundaries isn't welcome. Like anywhere else, close, friendly relationships are built naturally by spending time with people with whom you get on well. And once you call someone a friend in Kazakhstan, you must be genuinely prepared to grant favors and provide the kind of help that might be seen as excessive in other cultures: to lend money, to let your friend live in your house for as long as he or she might need to, and to be available whenever the person needs you, regardless of your job or your other plans. Certainly, you would not do such things for a person who hasn't won your full trust—who is not a real friend.

ATTITUDES TOWARD FOREIGNERS

As a foreigner in Kazakhstan you are likely, overall, to experience a friendly and warm reception. In the countryside, where the tradition of hospitality to a stranger is still the norm, you are likely to be treated in a special way, with invitations thrown at you the very minute you meet a new person. Even though this does not apply in the bigger cities, you are still likely to feel comfortable there among the locals, with little likelihood of experiencing any hostility. On the streets, people may stare at you, behave cautiously, be skeptical, or seem a bit rude, but aggressive attitudes are extremely rare. This doesn't mean that there are no thieves and beggars, of course, and commonsense vigilance is always advisable.

In urban areas you may sometimes encounter a small degree of anti-Americanism. The image of the United States has suffered since the invasion of Iraq in 2003, but there are certainly no extremes. The worst-case scenario may involve blunt questions about your attitude toward US foreign policy. In the countryside, however, where people have little interest in politics or foreign affairs, you are first and foremost a guest. This means you will be treated with the utmost respect and care, though jokes about spies may be made. These date from Soviet times, when every foreigner was considered a spy.

Young people, who have the most open-minded and unprejudiced attitudes, particularly those who speak English, are especially ready to make foreign friends. In the workplace, with its mixture of ages and backgrounds, attitudes vary. Building friendships can, as we have seen, take years, and there is also a stereotypical attitude that in the West friendship (in the Kazakh understanding) is superficial.

Another common belief is that all Western visitors and expats are excessively rich. Taxi drivers, hotel bellboys, and other service staff will expect you to pay or tip much more generously than a local customer. The less likely they are to see you again, the more likely you are to be cheated. Idealizing life in the West is also very common.

If you want to make friends in Kazakhstan, the best advice is to learn some of the language— Russian if you will be staying in a city, or Kazakh if you will be based in the country. This is of great importance to your acclimatization, and will endear you to the locals. As one foreign visitor with lots of Kazakh and Russian friends put it, "Ask everyone you know to be your teacher, and use whatever you can pick up. The more you are willing to look bad, make mistakes, and try, the more people will realize that you value them and their culture."

INVITATIONS HOME

Kazakhs have always held guests in high regard. Hospitality is one of the main national characteristics, displayed at its best in Kazakh *auls* (villages) in the countryside. Here children learn hospitality and respect from a young age.

If you visit a rural Kazakh family, whether or not you are expected, everyone will stand up to greet you as you enter. You will be seated on the *tor,* the special guest seat, and offered tea and biscuits, *baursaks* (donuts), and sweets. Traditional etiquette requires your host to remain silent until you have been refreshed. You will be genuinely welcome to stay on for a meal, if you are not in a hurry, and if you are breaking a journey you will be invited to stay overnight, or even for several days. If the family's circumstances allow, they will slaughter an animal (usually a lamb or a sheep) to serve you the traditional dish of *beshbarmak* (see page 107), and will want to make sure you are well fed and comfortable throughout your stay. This doesn't mean that a complete stranger can enter any house in any village and expect such treatment, but you are unlikely to be turned away if you find yourself in difficult circumstances for some reason.

In the cities things are much more formal, and people don't usually visit others at home without an invitation, or without letting the host know that they are coming. If you show up at short notice you will be served tea and snacks, and if expected you will probably be served a proper meal.

If it's a special occasion, expect a feast. Usually, as many guests are invited as will fit around the host's table, and you are likely to spend most of the time there. A selection of starters will be served, followed by one or two main dishes, then, after a break, tea and sweet dishes. Expect to be completely stuffed by the end of it, as whenever your plate looks less than mountainous with food, the hosts will pile on some more. The same will happen with the drink in your glass, so  one has to be careful not to get drunk. Strong drinks, such as vodka and cognac, are not drunk without a toast (see below), but sipping wine during the meal is fine. If your hosts know you are a vegetarian, they are likely to prepare separate food for you, which you must eat. Not eating the food provided is offensive.

Topics of Conversation

The atmosphere at the table will vary, depending on how well the guests know each other, but conversation is usually spontaneous and lively. There are no strict rules about topics. Popular subjects are children, their health and education, the family, health and healing, popular TV shows and programs, real estate and other prices, cars, road traffic, and football. One-on-one conversations usually start with talking about each other's families. Most local people are quite open about their personal lives and circumstances, and expect frankness in return. Perhaps the only area that is considered to be too private to be discussed, and better avoided, is sexual activity, but there are few taboos, even on topics such as politics and corruption.

Having said that, a foreigner should of course be aware that mocking the local culture, traditions, and way of life is likely to be perceived as disrespectful, and criticizing the local political situation is seen as patronizing. However, as long as you show your hosts that you respect them and value your stay in Kazakhstan, your conversation is unlikely to embarrass them.

Toasting

This is an important part of every festivity. The host or a chosen guest will take on the role of toastmaster. He (or in rare cases she) will then give the other guests a turn. Every guest is given a chance to propose a toast, and this should be taken.Not being invited to propose a toast is seriously offensive. The order of toasts is determined by age, social position, and relationship to the host (for example, *kudalar*, or in-laws, are always given priority over other family members). Every toast follows a short introduction from the toastmaster.

Kazakhs love long toasts, which may include jokes, proverbs, poems, and songs. Guests are expected to say at least a few words about the hosts. The simplest outline of a toast could be as follows: tell the other guests how you have come to know the hosts, praise their hospitality and generosity, and make an elaborate declaration of your best wishes to them and the family.

After each toast everyone drinks, and not to do so is rude. Vodka and cognac are the most popular spirits. If you don't drink alcohol, it is acceptable to imitate drinking each toast, but the toastmaster or host will watch—this is one of the local hospitality rules—and if he insists on your drinking, be ready with a good excuse, best related to some sort of health problem, which will be understood. A more gentle approach could be to sip rather than gulp.

ENTERTAINING

Other means of entertaining may include taking you out to a restaurant, family banquets, sightseeing trips, picnics, or a visit to a theater, opera, or ballet. Your hosts will expect to pay, so don't insist on sharing the cost; this may be considered offensive.

If you are doing the entertaining you are free to follow your own rules of hospitality and etiquette, as accepting your way of doing things is also part of the local culture of hospitality. Just bear in mind that if you have invited your friends to a restaurant or anywhere else, you will be expected to pay.

Once you are settled in the country, especially if you have a family, you might want to reciprocate with invitations to people or families who have already entertained you at their homes or elsewhere. This is certainly a rule among locals, but as a foreigner you are considered a guest in the country, and are free to choose whether of not to comply without fear of causing offense to your local friends.

If you have invited friends home, make sure that you will have plenty of supplies. Running out of food and drink to serve your guests is considered shameful.

DATING

Although Kazakh society is predominantly traditional, attitudes toward young people dating and building relationships are largely open and unprejudiced. There are exceptions, such as being in a serious relationship with someone of a different nationality. Homosexual relationships are likely to face even less tolerance, indeed close to zero. But other than that, people are free to choose whom they date, for how long, and at what personal distance. And even though girls are raised to believe that ideally they are to date one man, fall in love with him, and eventually marry him, foreign values of being in free relationships are gradually taking hold, especially among the younger generation in the cities. Paradoxically, it is easier for foreigners to make friends through dating than through other activities.

Social networking has become a common starting point preceding dating. A typical scenario nowadays for the development of romantic relationships involves meeting each other via a social network, then going out to a café or bar. The initiative usually comes from the male side, and it is the man who usually pays the bill, although on the first date the girl may insist on paying her share. Bringing flowers to the first date used to be common in the past, but this is now characteristic of a more serious relationship.

SOME SMALL POINTS OF ETIQUETTE

- Invitations may be extended well in advance, or with just a day's notice.
- Dressing up for the occasion is common.
- You are not expected to arrive exactly on time, but being more than thirty minutes late is rude.
- Gifts are usually given to the hostess. Bring small presents for her and any children, or buy a box of chocolates or biscuits; also bring a bottle of wine, especially if it is your first visit.
- Once over the threshold (step over it with your right foot), you will be greeted by the host, who shakes hands with male guests, using both hands.
- Take off your coat and shoes. Make sure that your shoes are placed the right way up. You will be offered slippers, but you can decline them, or you can bring your own if you wish.
- Whistling in a house and blowing your nose in public are considered bad manners.
- Leaving early isn't normal, and may offend your hosts. Wait until after the tea stage, and then you can start saying good-bye. Parties running late into the night are quite common.
- Don't refuse the *sarkyt*, which are small portions of food from the festive table (*dastarkhan*) that you may be given to take home with you.
- It is not necessary to send a thank-you card or letter after a party in someone's home.

chapter five

AT HOME

We have seen that the family is central to all Kazakhstanis, large family networks being especially valued by the Kazakhs and other Muslim communities. Because of this, most daily life takes place at home rather than in public places such as restaurants, malls, and parks. Even during office lunch hours most workers hurry home, or to the nearest close relative, to share a meal and socialize a little. In rural areas people are even more family oriented, with almost no outside entertainment options. Students and young people living in cities are possibly the only exception, spending most of their time away from home and preferring the company of their friends.

HOUSING

As in other parts of the former Soviet Union, most city dwellers in Kazakhstan live in big concrete apartment blocks. These were built during Soviet times as state-owned apartments that were allotted rent-free to workers through their factories, research centers, municipal offices, and so on. Later, after the USSR collapsed, all apartments were privatized and signed over to their occupants at very low or no cost. This type of housing doesn't look very attractive, and is fairly standard in terms of space, with a maximum

of three bedrooms, but they all have amenities and utilities such as a central heating system, gas, water, and electricity. It is worth mentioning that Soviet-style central heating means you can't turn the heat on and off as you wish: it is turned on by the state heating company in mid-October each year and turned off in mid-April without regard to the temperatures outside, and radiators can't be controlled from inside the apartment. Utility services, along with cleaning and lighting of shared spaces and courtyards, are managed by an association of apartment owners, known as a KSK. These apartments vary in age, construction, and layout, which together determine their market price.

In the 2000s some of the larger cities, especially Almaty and Astana, saw a major construction boom, driven by unprecedented internal and external investment into the country's banking sector. The financial crisis of 2008 left many of those housing construction projects unfinished. Even so, nearly a decade of real estate development significantly

expanded housing options for the urban middle and upper classes. The latter prefer elite town houses in the picturesque areas of Almaty, or luxury apartments in the newly built glittering skyscrapers of Astana. Smaller towns, however, have seen little of the real estate boom, with people still stuck in grey, often crumbling, Soviet-era blocks.

Villages across the country usually consist of small, two-to-three-roomed, single-story, detached houses, painted white and blue. Even during the Soviet era these were mostly privately owned, though construction was carried out or supervised by local authorities and thus there was no excessive decorative or architectural innovation. Very few houses were allowed to be more than one story high. Typically, such dwellings tend to lack modern facilities and are not connected to the sewage system. Bigger villages and small towns represent a mixture of multifamily apartment blocks and single-family detached houses. To a Kazakhstani, living in a house is considered to be the less desirable option, because of the lack of amenities and shortage of space. This does not apply to the wealthy people of the bigger cities, who build expensive mansions on the outskirts, contrasting with small groups of cramped, shabby, rural-type houses scattered in and outside the same cities.

THE HOUSEHOLD

The contrast between rural and urban home life in Kazakhstan is truly great. In the countryside several generations of a family are accustomed to living under one roof, following the tradition of *ata-balasy* mentioned earlier. Grandparents often look after small children while the parents are at work. This is seen as normal, because of another old tradition of *baurga basu* (literally, "pressing to the liver," or cuddling the baby), according to which an older child is often given away to grandparents to be raised as their own until the age of five or six. Such a child is then thought to be "special," as he or she has had an opportunity to absorb the grandparents' wisdom and has thus grown to be a wiser, more responsible, and more mature person than his or her siblings. Today the tradition is useful when poverty drives young parents to move from the countryside to the towns and cities, leaving the children behind.

City Kazakhs are less traditional. They have mixed with Slavs long enough to seem almost European in their home life. It is less common for young couples to join the parents, with brides preferring to have independent households of their own. Lack of space in city apartments often serves as a good enough excuse. Wealthier families,

however, may have enough space, so the question of living under one roof is back on the agenda, creating a great deal of tension between the in-laws.

Improvements in the quality of urban life and living conditions have also had an effect on the birthrate. Many couples now prefer to have more children, exceeding the urban norm of two. Families with three or four children are becoming more common in the cities. A government-sponsored program to boost the birthrate has also had its effect. A working pregnant woman can take up to a year of partially paid maternity leave, sponsored by the government, receives substantial financial aid at the birth, and is entitled to unpaid leave from her job until the child is three years of age. In contrast, nonworking women enjoy fewer benefits. Unemployed and generally poor families in the countryside tend to have fewer children than the usual five to eight that were typical during pre-Soviet and Soviet periods of Kazakh history.

THE DAILY ROUND

Most offices are open from 9:00 a.m. to 6:00 p.m.;
some from 10:00 a.m. to 7:00 p.m. Working overtime
is common in most private companies and
systematic for all government ministries in Astana.
Large food stores and little corner shops may be open
twenty-four hours; medium-sized stores tend to
open at 10:00 a.m. The lunch hour in most private
companies and government offices is between 1:00
and 2:00 p.m. Western companies practice a more
flexible approach, offering employees the choice of
taking their lunch hour any time between 12:00 noon
and 3:00 p.m. In bigger cities such as Almaty and
Astana traffic is heavy between 8:30 and 10:00 a.m.
and 6:30 and 8:00 p.m.

EVERYDAY SHOPPING

Major food stores are available for customers from
8:00 or 9:00 a.m. until 10:00 p.m. Some are in the
main streets of towns and cities, and others are
located on the outskirts. All are open seven days a
week, and some are open twenty-four hours a day.
Because stores stay open late in the evening, and
also because many local food products do not
contain preservatives, food shopping is usually
done on a daily basis, or two or three times a week.

A foreign visitor should note that many
supermarkets don't cater to foreigners or gourmands,
and for certain items like sauces, spices, tortillas,
and so on, you need to go to specific stores, such as
Ramstor and Interfood, that target foreigners, label
everything in English, and may have English-
speaking staff.

RAFAEL'S DAY

To give an idea of what a day is like for an office worker, here is an account by Rafael, a thirty-three-year-old sales manager working for a chain of grocery stores.

"My usual wake-up time is 8:00 a.m. I rush into the shower, get dressed, kiss my wife and five-year-old son, and head to the office. I live near the city's downtown, so it is only a fifteen-minute drive by car. If the traffic is heavy it may take up to thirty minutes, and on such days I am five or ten minutes late, which isn't considered critical here provided you don't come late on a daily basis. Once at the office I make myself a cup of instant coffee (the coffee machine broke recently but the office admin refuses to get it fixed, pointing to the recent budget cuts), go to my desk, and check my mail. The working day begins with phone calls and correspondence, followed by brief inspection visits to the company's stores.

"On my way back to the office, after noon, I buy something to eat from a small corner shop that sells packed meals, the local version of a takeaway that you can heat in a microwave. If I am lucky and not too pressed for time, I meet my wife near her office (she also works at the city center) to have a proper lunch together in a restaurant. They offer set lunches for a discount price.

My typical working day usually finishes just after 6:00 p.m., but if there is a meeting or an urgent task to finish then I stay for another hour or two. Working overtime two or three times a week is not a problem provided it doesn't happen on a daily basis.

Then I pick up my son from the kindergarten. We pop into the local corner shop to buy bread and fresh vegetables, and then we go home and wait for Mom to return from work. Once she's home we have dinner, which she has usually prepared the day before. This is the main meal of the day. It's a special time for all of us as we talk a lot, sharing news and making plans.

Then I grab my laptop to check my e-mail and social network accounts, and have brief online chats with friends. My wife does the dishes and cooks food for tomorrow while the little one goes to his room to play for a while. I join him later while my wife takes her turn at the laptop. They both go to sleep at 11:00 p.m. I stay up a little longer to surf the Internet, reading news and blogs and downloading music and videos.

We do our main food shopping once every two weeks at large supermarkets on the outskirts of Almaty. They are good for buying household cleaning materials and small food items such as juices, canned and pickled food, sausages, basic dairy products, cookies, and candies. At our local open market we buy meat and poultry from a seller recommended to us by neighbors for good-quality meat."

For fresh fruits, vegetables, and dried fruit and nuts (very popular), and sometimes for meat and fish, people go to local or central markets, where they can buy fresh produce more cheaply than in supermarkets, and often direct from the farmers. Saturdays and Sundays are busy market days. For smaller quantities of fruits and vegetables you can turn to the many little open street stalls scattered around the city, usually until 7:00 or 8:00 p.m.

Small corner shops sell milk and other dairy products, bread, sausages, cooking oil, sweets, cigarettes, beer, juice, and various other items. The quality and choice in these stores vary, but they are useful if you have forgotten to get something at the supermarket, and many of them are open around the clock. It is also worth mentioning that in most of these stores almost everything is behind the counter, so if you can't see what you want you will need to ask the cashier for it.

Smaller stores run out of certain products often, and not everything is available all the time. Also you may find supermarket staff unhelpful. The exception is, again, the bigger stores in Almaty and Astana, but even there the language barrier can slow things down for visitors. In the smaller supermarkets and corner shops it is generally advisable to check the expiry dates on your purchases.

CHILDREN

As mentioned above, large families with at least five children used to be a tradition in Kazakh society. Nowadays families have become smaller, yet having children is a must. Young married couples who prefer to delay having children often face open disapproval from their families. Infertility— considered a great misfortune—becomes psychologically unbearable for couples with health problems, as the pressure from relatives and friends sympathizing and trying to help can be excessive. Many such couples break up, with very few resorting to adoption.

As we have seen, knowledge of ancestry and lineage is paramount for Kazakhs, so there is a great deal of prejudice against adoption. It has to be said, however, that abandoning babies is a new phenomenon that appeared in the course of the twentieth century. In the earlier days of nomadic tribal life, there were virtually no abandoned babies: orphans were adopted by other family or clan members, and cases of premarital pregnancy were promptly resolved by clan leaders, who forced the couples to marry. Today, as more young girls and boys from various parts of the country move to the big cities for study and work—unsupervised and sexually uneducated—the problem of abandoned babies is at a peak, and orphanages are growing in number. All such institutions are public and financed from the state budget.

In urban families, which are typically smaller than rural ones even with the changing trends, children are raised in hothouse conditions—they are showered with love and overprotected. Parents and especially grandparents are always vigilant in making sure that children are well fed, warmly dressed to the point of being overdressed, and kept away from any potential hazards. In the countryside, where bigger families are still the norm, such attitudes are more relaxed, and children grow up to be more adaptable and resilient—but they are also raised more strictly, to be obedient, to have the utmost respect for their elders, and to help about the house from an early age. In contrast, city families are much more democratic in their parenting styles, giving their children more freedom of choice.

There is one common feature between urban and rural families—the role of grandparents in raising children. In the countryside the first child and even younger siblings can be raised entirely by the grandparents. In cities this old tradition is now less popular, yet many grandparents still do most of the child rearing, especially after mothers go back to work. Most grandparents and their grandchildren stay close to each other through their lifetime, developing a very special relationship.

EDUCATION
Noncompulsory preschool education is provided by state and private kindergartens that give basic writing and reading classes. A one-year preparatory program

is also offered free of charge at most secondary schools. Once children reach the age of six (some parents prefer to wait until seven) they start school. A standard compulsory education is nine years, while high school students attend classes for eleven years. Free education is always available, and there are also plenty of private schools.

In most schools, classes take place in two or even three shifts because of a shortage of classrooms. In many rural schools there is also a lack of materials and the teachers are extremely badly paid, so parents commonly make small, illegal donations to schools.

School education is provided primarily in Kazakh (by Kazakh schools) and Russian (by Russian schools), with some schools using Uzbek, Uighur, or Tajik as their main teaching languages. There are eight private schools in the country that offer all classes in English. Kazakh-language schools predominate in the countryside, with more Russian-language schools in the towns and cities. Kazakh and Russian schools differ slightly in teaching methods and, many people think, in the quality of their education as well. Russian schools are regarded as being more advanced. There are also some differences in their education styles: Kazakh schools tend to pay more attention to discipline and less to the individual initiative of pupils; Russian schools are thought to be more democratic in style. As for youth culture, there is no strict segregation between teenagers studying at Kazakh and Russian schools, but there might be rivalry between those living in different city districts. Also, urban and rural youth don't get along easily.

Having said that, the curriculum is universal for both Russian and Kazakh schools, and thus the similarities are greater than the differences mentioned. The primary focus is on mathematics, science, history, and languages. Kazakh and Russian grammar and literature are obligatory. Hardly any importance is attached to arts, music, and sports, and children having a particular interest in any of these are forced out of secondary schools to apply to specialized colleges. The relationships between teachers and pupils are usually very formal, especially in Kazakh schools. Unfortunately, this doesn't make for a creative attitude toward the learning process or encourage initiative. It doesn't mean, however, that there is a lack of enthusiasm among pupils. Most people—and their children—are very serious about education.

At the end of grade 11 high school pupils take their final examinations (the ENT, or United National Test) in five disciplines: mathematics, Kazakh, Russian, Kazakh history, and one elective

subject in science, the humanities, or a foreign language. The results determine entry to universities, where getting a degree used to take five years, with the possibility of an extension toward a doctorate. Now most universities offer a four-year bachelor's degree with an optional two-year postgraduate course to follow.

Being a student in Kazakhstan is not hard. The family usually pays for tuition, and the student just has to make sure that he or she meets the minimum requirements to finish a course. Standards for financially secure students aren't very high. Most students start working while at the university and can afford bribes to teachers in case they can't juggle work and study. Corruption in higher education is endemic, with only a handful of universities committed to meeting internationally recognized standards. For a student the problem reveals itself later, when the graduate realizes that he or she is not adequately qualified to compete in the labor market.

HEALTH CARE
This is a sector that has gone through continuous reform since independence. Currently, every taxpayer is entitled to free public health care, but this is delivered somewhat differently in rural and urban areas. In country areas, primary care is delivered through medical clinics, *feldsher* (midwifery) units, and small hospitals. In urban areas, primary care is delivered by polyclinics, or general clinics. These are big medical facilities, separate for adults and children, with ten to twenty professionals such as general physicians, pediatricians, and gynecologists. Most have laboratories on site.

Basic secondary care is delivered by district (*rayon*) hospitals, with more specialized secondary care in regional (*oblast* or city) hospitals, and tertiary care in national specialist institutes. Throughout the system the tendency has been to refer patients to a higher level of care. This delivery system is in the process of being reorganized, and the eventual goal is for primary care to be delivered by family physicians.

There is a twenty-four-hour emergency service available in free-standing or hospital-based ambulance units. The staff teams consist of physicians, midwives, and nurses, with specialist backup, such as cardiologists. Patients call an emergency phone number and a physician decides whether the patient can be treated at home or should be taken to a polyclinic or a hospital. Post-treatment information is sent to the patient's physician or family doctor. In smaller towns the emergency units have too few or poorly maintained ambulances, sometimes without enough gas to take people to the hospital, and they also lack medicine and equipment. Patients often have to be transported some distance, as not all hospitals provide emergency care.

The sector has been struggling for many years due to the underfunding of hospitals, clinics, and staff salaries, especially in rural areas. As with the education sector, bribery is commonplace. Unofficial payments for shorter operation wait times, longer hospital stays, and better-quality care are extremely widespread. Yet public health care is the only option available within the country in the case of serious illness. The private health care sector—although it has grown considerably—is still very small. It typically covers most pharmacies and dentists, and can provide primary and basic secondary care services. However, the government is now promoting voluntary health care insurance, which has been taken up by some large businesses, especially in the financial services and energy sectors. Cost-wise, local private health care is much cheaper than in Western countries.

In public clinics doctors don't usually make appointments, which means that patients have to wait in line. Another peculiarity worth mentioning is the over-cautious attitude toward health, among both doctors and the public in general. For example, diagnosis of the smallest problem is taken very seriously, with people sent for many different tests that may reveal a set of other problems. All will then be treated with a great deal of medicine—much more than would be prescribed in the West.

In addition to conventional medicine, folk remedies and alternative medicine are extremely popular in Kazakhstan, along with healers of all kind – herbalists, psychics, or simply shamans, known locally as *baksy*. Specialized magazines and TV programs dedicated to these alternatives attract great numbers of readers and viewers across the country. Furthermore, after the fall of the USSR, when trade gates were opened, the country was swept by salesmen from abroad, building a wide distribution network for products that apparently bring ultimate cures for all sorts of health problems. In recent years, homeopathy and Chinese medicine have been on the rise. All of these work through personal recommendation.

chapter six

TIME OUT

Kazakhstanis in general have a generous two-to-
three-week vacation each year, which they usually
spend with their families, visiting relatives, or
traveling to beauty spots or health resorts. Time out,
Kazakh-style, is all about entertaining and being
entertained—getting together with family and
friends. Dinners at home with at least a dozen
guests, birthday parties in a restaurant, and bigger
celebrations, called *tois*, are all typical ways of
spending weekends and holidays. The parties are
all alike in their essence, with a great deal of eating
(mainly of *beshbarmak*—see below), drinking
(mainly of vodka), toasting (the longer the better),
and dancing—the ultimate indicator of a party's
success. On the rare occasions when there is no

birthday or wedding to celebrate, leisure hours may be spent on cultural pursuits, sports, and outdoor activities. Then, of course, there is the Friday night phenomenon: nothing beats a glass of beer with your close circle of friends at a café, bar, or restaurant.

EATING OUT

The Kazakh diet has been heavily influenced by the traditionally nomadic way of life. Authentic Kazakh food involves meat—mutton, beef, and horsemeat. The quintessentially Kazakh dish is *beshbarmak*, which is pieces of slow-cooked meat served with flat squares of pasta and chopped boiled onions. The meat stock is drunk separately but is considered part of the dish. Some other popular dishes—*plov*

(stir-fried rice with mixed vegetables and meat), *laghman* (long noodles in a beef and vegetable soup) and *manty* (steamed meat mixture dumplings)—are of wider Central Asian origin and not exclusive to Kazakhstan. Russian cuisine has also been part of the local flavor for long enough to become integral to the general Kazakh family diet: *pirozhki* (small pies with various fillings), *bliny* (thin pancakes), *pelmeni* (little round dumplings filled with meat), and pickled tomatoes and cucumbers are favorites in every home.

There is no shortage of restaurants, most of which offer a mix of Russian and Central Asian food, though the best local cuisine will be found in private homes. In the bigger cities eating out has been popular long enough for restaurant fare to rival traditional homemade dishes. At the upper end are international restaurants, with Italian and French being the most popular. Turkish and Georgian restaurants offer less expensive, heartier portions, and thus are great for family dinners. The popularity of Chinese, Japanese, and Middle Eastern cuisine is also on the rise, but most would struggle to survive on serving such exotic food alone, so they offer local dishes too.

Popularity in Kazakhstan seldom means that a restaurant is packed, so a reservation is not normally necessary, even in the biggest cities. Overcrowded places are rare, with the exception of restaurants that serve a set lunch, and the most popular bars on a Friday night. Having breakfast out is not in the local culture, and cafés serving early breakfasts are found only in Almaty's city center, catering to tourists.

When eating out in Kazakhstan the main difficulties for the foreign visitor are usually the lack of menus in English and the lack of an English-speaking wait staff. Thus many foreigners just order by pointing to random items on the menu. What you may find pleasing, however, is that you can always count on having a hot meal, whether you're in a coffee shop, café, restaurant, or bar. Alcoholic drinks are usually available as well. Water does not come free, and asking for tap water isn't common.

For a quick hot snack, nothing beats the students' favorite, the small twenty-four-hour *döner* shops, where you get a *döner kebab* (small pieces of grilled lamb or chicken) wrapped in a roll of thin *lavash* (tortilla-like bread), with sliced carrot and sour cream. Turkish-style fast-food cafés, budget *laghman* places, and small pizza stops are another good option. Many local fast-food restaurants are located in shopping malls, alongside international chains such as KFC.

Most eateries, including coffee shops and cafés, are open from noon until very late at night. Just note that if a restaurant or a café carries a name in English, German, or any other language (except perhaps Chinese), it doesn't necessarily mean that the staff will speak that language.

Credit cards are accepted in most international restaurants, yet Kazakhstan is still a predominantly cash society. Foreign currency isn't accepted, so make sure you have enough Kazakh tenge with you when you go out. ATMs are available at banks and supermarkets.

NIGHTLIFE

Even the big cities in Central Asia don't really buzz as you might hope. Undoubtedly, the best place to have a night out in Kazakhstan is Almaty. Evening entertainment venues are scattered around the city, and although there is not much variety there are several to choose from. New themed bars, lounges, and discos are cropping up, while many of the old ones are making changes to accommodate the city's vibrant student presence and twenty-somethings, as well as a richer, thirty-plus clientele. The number of professional DJs is growing, bringing the city's club culture on to a new level, and there are frequent festivals, special music events, and parties. The annual Ibiza Mega Dance outside the city at Lake Kapchagai is the most popular of all, featuring DJs from Western Europe.

Astana is a beautiful place at night, with its illuminated modern architecture. Its bar and club scene is gradually developing, and there are several options offered, such as, for example, a disco called Shokolad (Chocolate), popular with local folk, Guns N'Roses Café, which has live music, and the new Mojo bar, with its more sophisticated decor. In other parts of the country, Shymkent could be the choice for those who want to taste southern-Kazakh-style hospitality. The combination of delicious Uzbek

TIPPING

A 10 percent service charge is added to a restaurant bill, and on top of that you are usually expected to tip the waiter. However, the tip does go to the individual rather than into a shared fund. Depending on the quality of service, you can tip 5 to 15 percent. Leaving no tip for the waiter is acceptable if you feel the service wasn't satisfactory.

Tipping taxi drivers—especially unofficial ones—isn't common. You simply bargain and agree on your fare before boarding the taxi, and that is it. If, however, you have heavy luggage that requires the driver's help, or if you ask for additional favors on your way (such as stopping at a cash machine or a corner shop), or if you find the driver is helpful in answering questions and giving practical advice, then giving him an additional 500 to 1,000 tenge (approximately 3 to 6 US dollars) is a good and generous way to thank him.

The same principle applies to tipping hotel staff. If someone on the administrative staff is particularly helpful throughout your stay, you can tip up to 5,000 tenge (30 US dollars), or even give a small gift, with a smile and a few words of appreciation. As for cleaning and other support staff, there are no rules.

In city centers, when parking a car on the street, you will be helped by people in a yellow or blue uniform, and you will be expected to tip them 50 to 100 tenge. On trains, *marshrutkas*, buses, and planes, however, there is no tipping.

cuisine and cheap drinks makes this city especially attractive to students from all over the country.

Late-night cinema is another favorite of Kazakhstan's city folk. Hollywood movies dubbed into Russian form the main repertoire. In Almaty there is an IMAX cinema at Essentai Mall and another cinema (Tsezar) specializing in art-house films. Some art movies are also screened at the Arman cinema in Astana's Aziapark mall.

Gambling is legal in Kazakhstan, but only in special zones. The legal casinos are located either on the shore of Lake Kapchagai near Almaty or at Lake Borovoe in the north of the country. These zones aren't really popular, and much of the business has gone underground in the cities. Both Almaty and Astana are generously sprinkled with illegal gambling halls.

CULTURAL LIFE
Music
The Kazakhstani love of the classical arts was nurtured during the Soviet period. In the major cities—especially Almaty and Astana—there are

plenty of opportunities to see opera, ballet, and concerts of classical music and more. In Almaty, look out for performances at the Abay Opera House (110 Kabanbai Street; www.gatob.kz, Web site in Russian and Kazakh), which stages both Western and Kazakh opera such as *Kyz Zhibek* and *Abay*. There is also no shortage of classical, jazz, and other concerts at Kazakh Concert Hall (83 Ablay Khan Street), Kurmangazy Conservatory Hall (86 Ablay Khan Street; www.conservatoire.kz, Web site with limited English) and the State Philarmonia (35 Kaldayakov Street; www.fil.kz, Web site in Russian only), which also often puts on concerts of organ music. In the local classical music scene there are world-class performers, such as the Kamerata Kazakhstana chamber orchestra, the Bekova Trio, the violinists Marat Bisengaliyev and Ayman Musakhodjayeva, the pianist Zhaniya Aubakirova, and many others.

Astana has its own grand opera and ballet theater (www.astana.anshlag.kz, Web site with English) housed in a new majestic building in the administrative district of the city known as the Left

Bank. Among other newly built halls there is the large Kazakhstan Central Concert Hall, with 3,500 seats, and the opera hall at the Pyramid of Peace (Palace of Peace and Reconciliation) designed by the English architect Sir Norman Foster.

Traditional folk music concerts should not be missed. Someone once called the Kazakh Steppe a "sea of music," with good reason. Vocal and instrumental music has played an enormous role in the lives of ordinary Kazakhs for centuries. You will be surprised at the variety of original Kazakh musical instruments, many of which have been revived since the fall of the Soviet Union. Chief among these is the *dombra*, a slender, long-necked, two-stringed lute. The *kobyz*, another ancient stringed instrument, is played with a bow, and is closer to the violin. Keep your eyes open for folk orchestras such as the Kurmangazy Orchestra, the Otrar Sazy Folk Orchestra, Sazgen, and Sybyzgy Sazy. They perform on a regular basis in Almaty and Astana concert halls, and also make frequent tours across the country.

Theater
Kazakhs and Russians alike are eager theatergoers. Since Kazakhstan is a bilingual country there are Russian theaters, where all plays are performed in Russian, and Kazakh theaters, where all are in Kazakh. There is an audio translation from Kazakh into Russian at Auezov Kazakh Theater in Almaty, and that is pretty much it. Unless you are a fluent Russian or Kazakh speaker you will not get much out of local theater.

Kazakh *aytis*—a musical–poetic duel based on improvization between two bards—is another local favorite, but this again is quite an isolating experience if you are not a fluent Kazakh speaker.

You may have difficulty in finding information about what is going on, when, and where. Most events are advertised in the local press in Russian, and some in Kazakh. A few Web sites, such as www.afisha.kz and www.timeout.kz, give a good overview, but again the main language used is Russian. Knowing the language, or having someone handy who knows it, is critical if you want to find information, or in fact to get anywhere, in Kazakhstan.

Visual Arts
There is a variety of art galleries and museums that will give the visitor an excellent insight into the country's astonishing traditional culture and modern arts. The Kasteyev State Museum of Art in Almaty (30A Satpayev Street; www.gmirk.kz, a Web site with some information in English) offers an exhaustive overview of paintings and sculptures by local artists, including a considerable collection by Abylkhan Kasteyev, the first professional Kazakh painter. A separate room displays Kazakh traditional handicrafts, including rugs, jewelry, and nomadic household utensils.

The best places in Almaty to see the work of modern artists are the Ular Gallery (92 Panfilov Street; www.artular.kz) of the Kazakhstan's Union of Professional Artists and the private Tengri Umay Gallery of Modern Art (103 Panfilov Street; www.tu.kz), which acts as a center for a wider regional area and holds frequent art events.

In Astana the Museum of Modern Art (at 3 Respublika Street; www.msi-astana.kz, Web site in Russian and Kazakh only) puts on frequent exhibitions of work by local contemporary artists. Its permanent collection is rather small but well worth a visit if Astana is your only stop in Kazakhstan. Some modern art is also on display on the top floor of the adjoining Presidential Culture Center. Its main attraction, however, is a section on Kazakh history, which, among other things, features examples of the magnificent gold and silver jewelry of the Sak period (approximately the fifth to the second century BCE) and a replica of the "Golden Man"—a costume of a Sak/Scythian warrior made of gold pieces. The original pieces were found at Esik, fifty kilometers from Almaty, in 1969. The Golden Man has become a symbol of modern Kazakhstan, and there are replicas in museums all over the country.

The best place for an overview of the country's history and culture is the Central State Museum in Almaty (44 Samal-1; www.csmrk.kz; this Web site's

English version is not updated regularly). It houses a large collection of archaeological finds, weaponry, horse gear, clothes, and more. There are also a number of souvenir shops that sell traditional carpets. A visit to the Museum of Folk Musical Instruments is another must if you are in Almaty, especially if you don't have a chance to listen to traditional Kazakh music at a concert, because you will be able to hear some of these instruments being played at the museum.

SPORTS AND OUTDOOR ACTIVITIES

The Kazakh love of football was inherited from Soviet times. There is a joke that the number one national sport is watching football, and, indeed, most Kazakhstanis are now devoted fans of the leading English, Italian, and Spanish clubs. Playing amateur football is very popular, especially on weekends, with frequent tournaments between various amateur teams. Kazakhstan's national football has seen lots of sponsoring, but on the international football scene the country is struggling.

Ice hockey is another spectator sport that has long been popular in Kazakhstan, unlike professional cycling, in which interest has been generated over the last decade or so by the international Astana cycling team. The team has achieved impressive results at world level, and is heavily sponsored by a number of government-owned Kazakh companies.

The most popular active sports around Almaty are skiing and snowboarding—natural for a city lying within a thirty-minute drive of the mountains. There are four ski resorts near Almaty, with Chimbulak being the best equipped, most popular, and most expensive. The skiing season lasts from late October through April. Ice-skating is a favorite and less expensive pastime of Almaty dwellers in winter, and the Medeu ice rink just outside the city is one of the largest speed-skating rinks in the world. The Astana and Karagandy plains, and especially the Altai Mountains in the northeast of the country, are renowned for cross-country skiing.

The sporting preferences of those with money to spare often depend on the interests of President

Nazarbayev and his close circle. His favorites—golf, tennis, and skiing—are now the most popular with the Kazakh elite. One sport that has always been popular is the Russian version of billiards, which uses fifteen numbered white balls and one red. The balls are big, which makes it difficult to get them into the smaller pockets of the Russian billiard table, and, all in all, it is quite a demanding game.

The Tien Shan and Altai mountains also offer great opportunities for hiking. Areas around Almaty, certain spots between Shymkent and Taraz, and Rakhmanovskie Kluchi in the northeast of the country are best for that purpose. In warmer seasons the Ili River, north of Almaty, offers easy rafting and canoeing. All of these are especially popular with local Russians who love an active type of leisure, and pretty well everyone—Russians, Kazakhs, and others—loves fishing and simply picnicking.

Gyms are very popular, and vary in price from 50 to 500 US dollars a month, depending on the facilities they offer. Finally, yoga has made its way into local minds, especially women's. In most cities there is a wide choice of yoga classes available.

SHOPPING FOR PLEASURE

Southern Kazakhstan once prospered from the
historic Silk Road, a trading corridor between China
and Europe, and the modern markets and bazaars in
the south are reminiscent of that earlier trading
spirit. The Green Market in Almaty is probably the
closest reminder of the fabled route, and its main hall
is an impressive sight. There are rows of stands laden
with dried and fresh fruit and vegetables, herbs,
massive chunks of meat, fish, flowers, honey, and
ready-made "Korean" salads, which are much
appreciated locally. Seeing large quantities of caviar
on a market stall might take you by surprise—a
pleasant one, if you look at the prices and remember
those at home. A lower hall has more stalls of fruits
and vegetables, nuts, cheese, sausages, and dairy
products. Outside you can find clothes and pretty
much everything else, including small workshops
for the repair of shoes and clothing.

If you want a bargain, go to Almaty Barakholka,
on the outskirts of the city, which is known for its
sensationally low prices on everything from food to
furs. Bargaining is appropriate, and if you are lucky
enough to be accompanied by a local friend make
the most of it: try not to expose your foreign origin
to the seller, or you may push up the price!

Elsewhere in Almaty, and in fact in the whole of
Kazakhstan, shopping is rather expensive in
comparison to the rest of Central Asia, especially
neighboring China. For luxury international brands
such as Gucci, Dolce and Gabbana, Burberry, Fendi,
Louis Vuitton, and many more, go to the newly
opened Essentai Mall in Almaty. It also houses the
American department store Saks Fifth Avenue. For a
less pretentious shopping experience try the "trade

and entertainment centers" in most of the major cities. Astana's shopping centers are very popular with the locals, especially in winter, for they offer much more than just a shopping experience. The recently opened Khan Shatyr (The Khan's Tent) is more like a city than a shopping center, complete with its own beach resort. Yet Kazakhstan can hardly be called a shopper's paradise, with its slightly overpriced market and limited range of choice.

Souvenir shops can be found in all major hotels, shopping centers, and the large museums in Astana and Almaty. In Almaty the artisans' guild organizes a

market of Central Asian handicrafts on the last weekend of each month in front of the Zhetisu Hotel (55 Ablay Khan Street). During the warm season Sheber Aul, a handicraft community in Kokshoky, on the road to the Big Almaty Lake, is worth a visit. This community, in the picturesque setting of the Tien Shan, aims to support and promote traditional Kazakh handicrafts as a potentially profitable business. In Almaty, Zangar department store (formerly known as TSUM) also offers a good range of souvenirs, including felt rugs on the third floor. Nearby, on Zhibek Zholy Street, you can wander through a street market of oil paintings. Most are copies, and the prices will tell you that you aren't buying an authentic work of art, but you might find something you like for a souvenir.

SOME "MUST-SEE" ATTRACTIONS
Khoja Ahmed Yassawi Mausoleum

The most interesting tourist attraction in Kazakhstan is the late-fourteenth-century mausoleum of Khoja Ahmed Yassawi in Turkestan, the present-day town in southern Kazakhstan that was built on the site of the ancient town of Yassi. Constructed on the orders of Tamerlane in honor of the twelfth-century Sufi mystic and Turkic poet Hodja Ahmet Jassawi, its vault, dome, and glazed tile ornamentation mark the beginning of the new Timurid style of architecture (see page 26). A two-hour drive away is the historic excavation site of the ancient town of Otyrar and a number of tomb–mausoleums (see right). All these attractions are around 600 miles (almost 1,000 km) from Almaty, so plan accordingly.

Kazakh Horse Games

The once nomadic Kazakhs give special significance to the horse, and the various competitions on horseback are greatly loved. Check the local hippodrome for contests open to the public on certain weekends and public holidays. The Almaty venue is the Central Hippodrome on Akhan Sery Street.

Nura Eagle Hunting Museum and the Charyn Canyon

There are a few people who still practice the traditional Kazakh art of training hunting eagles (*berkut*). You can meet some of them at the Nura Eagle Hunting Museum near Almaty on the way to the border with China, a popular road taking you to the Charyn Canyon. Contests in hunting with birds take place every year near here, and also in the Turgen Valley, near Almaty. Check with one of the local travel agencies. The famous canyon is an attraction in itself, presenting magnificent views of the rough gorges cleft by the Charyn River. Locals like to compare it with the Grand Canyon. The trip may cost you up to 200 US dollars, and takes a day.

The Kazakh Folk Orchestra

Keep an eye open for concerts by the orchestras that play Kazakh music on Kazakh instruments: the Otrar Sazy Folk Orchestra, the Kurmangazy Orchestra, the Sazgen, and the Sybyzgy Sazy. They regularly perform in both Almaty and Astana, and frequently tour within the country.

Kazakh Aul (Village)

Although the traditional Kazakh semi-nomadic way of life no longer exists, in summer you can find Kazakh yurts in many steppe valleys across the country and on mountain pastures. If, while on a journey, you see a yurt and would like to meet and visit its owners, you will be hospitably greeted. You are sure to be offered some tea or a bowl of *kumys*—the traditional Kazakh drink made of fermented horse milk—with some bread and sweets. A full stay at a Kazakh yurt can be arranged through a local travel agent.

The Steppe

You can barely claim to have visited Kazakhstan unless you have been out in the steppe. The steppe is the essence of everything Kazakh. If you flew into the country you will have seen it from the air and realized the vastness of it, but its full impact can be experienced only on the ground, with nothing but the sky and a sea of grass around you. A twenty-hour Almaty-to-Astana journey by train (not the high-speed one called Talgo) may suffice to give you the feeling of it. If you are an experienced traveler you may want to take a car trip through the steppes of central Kazakhstan, featuring, surprisingly, not just the grassland, but beautiful lakes, hills, and woods.

chapter seven

TRAVEL, HEALTH, & SAFETY

Kazakhstanis are very sociable, and on a long journey you can expect a lot of questions and conversation, sharing of food, and offers of help.

When planning your visit the first thing you should take into account is the size of the country and the huge distances between towns. Kazakhstan covers such a large area that it has two (formerly three) time zones. The climate, and therefore the weather, varies significantly across the country. Most importantly, traveling takes a lot of time, especially by road—most roads are in a far from perfect state.

For example, imagine a sightseeing trip from Almaty to the most famous attraction, the Hodja Ahmet Jassawi Mausoleum in Turkestan. It is a worthwhile trip, but it takes almost twenty hours by train, or twelve to fifteen hours by car, and if you fly it will still take another couple of hours to get to the site by road from Shymkent Airport. To make the most of the journey many tourists go on to the excavation site of the ancient city of Otyrar and the tomb–mosque of Arystan Baba who, according to legend, was Hodja Ahmet Jassawi's teacher. These are a further two hours' drive away on a poor road. All in all, it is long, tiresome journey, which is better broken into smaller parts. Having time and lots of energy are essential for travel in Kazakhstan.

INTERCITY TRAVEL
By Air
Flying is the most reliable and smoothest way to travel between Kazakhstan's larger cities. The local carrier, Air Astana, has a modern fleet of aircraft and serves a broad network. Smaller local airlines fly to other destinations within the country, but none of these operate in EU airspace. They are fine by Kazakh standards, and the only problem with air travel from a local perspective is the bad winter conditions, which often cause long delays.

By Train
Traveling by train is a good option, and provided you have the time is reasonably good value for money. A trip from Almaty to a town in western Kazakhstan takes nearly three days. Not all cities are directly linked by rail, which means changing trains. The two main types of train are Talgo Express and standard.

Talgo Express trains run direct, nonstop, between the largest cities (Almaty to Taraz and Shymkent, and Almaty to Karagandy, Astana, Kokshetau, and Petropavlovsk).

Standard trains are of two types: "fast" and "passenger." The fast trains have fewer stops and provide better on-board service. Within these there are three classes to suit personal comfort, privacy, and budgeting: *SV* (special wagon), with two berths per cabin; *kupe*, with four berths per cabin (two above and two below); and *platskarta*, which are rows of berths along an open corridor.

To buy tickets you must show your passport (you will also need it to board the train), and pay with cash. At a local station this is best done in advance, because it can be quite a challenging experience, with offhand staff and long, chaotic lines. In the bigger cities a number of offices around town sell tickets in a less stressful atmosphere for a small commission.

Every train has a restaurant car—a communal eating place with a limited menu, always crowded and sometimes dangerous, as strong alcohol is always available. Between the carriages are smoking areas, and if you want to move from one carriage to another it is hard to avoid breathing in smoke.

Bed linen will be brought to you by the *provodnik* (attendant), who will deal with all the practicalities of the journey and may offer to make you tea—for a tip.

By Bus

Most intercity roads in Kazakhstan have a single carriageway. They aren't generally bad, but there are always a few parts of every road that are in need of serious repair. These and other factors, such as the risky driving culture and the poor state of some of the vehicles, make road trips fairly unsafe.

Yet intercity shuttle buses are very popular, especially for distances up to about three hundred miles (500 km). They are much cheaper and faster than the train, and cover all destinations. However, for lengthy trips lasting more than five or six hours intercity shuttles are not nearly as comfortable or as safe as trains. For short trips of up to four or five hours minibuses (called *marshrutkas*) are a popular alternative. They are a little more expensive than the shuttles, but are faster. They wait outside bus and train stations, and set off when full.

Tickets can be bought at local bus stations or from the driver on board. In the latter case your ticket will not be refundable. If the shuttle or *marshrutka* breaks down on the way you will have to pay for a seat on another bus or minibus on the same route.

By Taxi

Like *marshrutkas*, private intercity taxis can be found outside bus and train stations and can be rented for sole occupancy or shared with other passengers. A seat in a shared taxi costs double the price of a seat in a *marshrutka*. Unlike intercity shuttles and *marshrutkas* most private taxis are not licensed public carriers, and you, the traveler, must understand that you are the one who takes the risk on the road. You have to be careful with your personal safety. A safer option is to hire a taxi from a local company, though this is more expensive.

GETTING AROUND TOWN

By Taxi

The best way to travel around the bigger cities is by taxi. Some belong to taxi companies, where the fare is set in advance, but there are also many private taxis. You simply raise your hand while standing on the roadside and within two or three minutes at least one "civilian" driver is likely to stop. However, you should understand the dangers of getting into a stranger's private car, especially at night, and a woman on her own is advised not to take this risk.

Neither official nor unofficial taxis have meters, and few can provide receipts. There are generally accepted unofficial tariffs, which you should try to find out from a local friend. You agree on the fare before getting into the car, which may involve some bargaining. A tip is not expected.

By Bus

As with intercity travel, the bus network in towns and cities is extensive, but it is hard to learn the routes if you are new to the place. City buses are very crowded during peak hours and don't stick to their timetables. People don't wait in line, and stopping between assigned stops is prohibited, so boarding a bus at busy times can be a daunting experience.

On the bus a conductor will collect your fare—which will be low—and answer questions (in Russian or Kazakh) about the route and timetable. Buses run less frequently after 9:00 p.m., and the latest you can catch one is around 11:00 p.m.

By Tram, Trolleybus, and Metro

Almaty has a small network of trams, with only two routes (reduced from the ten operating in their heyday), that give the city a certain charm. Trolleybuses were first introduced to Almaty in the 1940s as an ecologically friendly option, and they are much loved by the city's inhabitants. Unfortunately both trams and trolleybuses have become economically unviable, but they still run.

The Metro has just one line, which opened in 2011, and a second is under construction. With high ceilings and finely decorated walls, the Metro resembles that in Moscow—except for its limited coverage of the city. At present it is not the quickest way to get around Almaty.

By Car

In Almaty, Astana, Atyrau, and some other cities you can rent a car. Hiring a driver along with the car is the safest option and costs 100 to 150 US dollars a day, excluding fuel. For intercity journeys it is best to choose a four-wheel-drive vehicle because of the rough roads, which may have potholes and seasonal hazards, such as black ice. These cars are popular in Almaty and Astana, and visitors may be surprised to see so many massive vehicles driven by city motorists.

If you intend to drive yourself, you will need an international driver's license, but you can apply for a Kazakh license after six months' residence. You should know that the wearing of safety belts is obligatory in the front seats, but not in the rear seats—in fact many cars do not have rear seat belts.

Kazakhstani driving in general is rather aggressive. Many people buy driver's licenses illegally, without having passed a test, and this lowers the general standard and quality of driving, despite the numerous fines imposed. Therefore driving can be erratic, and you should be ready for sudden moves by cars around you, as well as the frequent use of horns and lights. Everyone seems to want to overtake. Occasionally you may be given a courteous flash, meaning that you are being given the right of way. Minor collisions on the road are usually settled informally with an offer of cash, or the guilty party pays directly for the repair.

Gas and service stations are not widespread outside cities and towns, so it is advisable to carry extra petrol cans for long journeys. The system of traffic signs has been improved since Soviet days, but is not up to European standards. Intercity roads are poorly lit at night, so beware of potholes and other possible hazards, such as animals on the road and stationary vehicles without warning lights. Also there is not always clear signage of road works and damaged roads. During strong snowfalls some intercity roads are closed for days, so if you are planning a trip during the winter it is important to check local news reports.

Between the cities there are small private roadside cafés and guesthouses. The quality and service vary, but most are simple, targeting truck drivers. Their facilities are generally very basic, often just consisting of a squat toilet; if you have to pay to use the facilities they will be less basic.

Buying a car in Kazakhstan is a tiresome business, with lots of bureaucracy. There is a lengthy procedure for registering the car with the state traffic police and notarizing the deal. This needs to be done with care, so be sure to check all the documentation that goes with the car, such as insurance and the tax invoice.

There is a policy of zero tolerance for drunk driving, which means that driving with a blood-alcohol level greater than zero is an offence. The intercity speed limit is 110 kmph (nearly 70 mph). In towns and cities it is usually 60 kmph (nearly 40 mph), unless there is a traffic sign telling you otherwise. For example, if you go under a bridge or into a tunnel, or if there is a school or kindergarten ahead, the speed limit will drop to 40 kmph (25 mph). There are a few speed cameras around larger cities, but rules are generally enforced by traffic police. If you are stopped for breaking a rule, your license will be taken away. Getting it back involves a visit to the local traffic police office to pay the fine, which takes a lot of time and money (fines are high). Many drivers prefer the easier and cheaper way of bribing officers. Unfortunately, bribery has become a part of the driving culture on the roads of Kazakhstan, despite numerous government and public attempts to stop it.

WHERE TO STAY

Kazakhstan is the most expensive country in Central Asia. In the cities of Almaty and Astana and the major towns the high cost of hotels doesn't necessarily translate into quality. At the top end are international chains—Hyatt, InterContinental, and Rixos—and there are the Radisson SAS in Astana and Holiday Inn in Almaty. There are mid-range and budget options, or you could try one of the health resorts, or sanatoriums, which can be booked through local travel agencies. Staying in a private home is another convenient option for a visiting family. The best way to find one of these is by looking in the local newspapers (if you can read Russian) or by going through a local real estate agency.

In provincial towns, Soviet-inspired establishments—which are not the most welcoming places—prevail, and in a remote area you are likely to be limited to a spartan hostel or nothing at all. Visitors, however, are not likely to be left without a roof over their heads, for traditional Kazakh hospitality still rules in the rural areas.

HEALTH

There is reasonably good free national health care for Kazakhstanis. Foreign visitors usually go to private clinics. Full travel and medical insurance, arranged before your visit, is recommended. Consult your own country's health authorities before your visit about vaccinations, especially if you will be coming for a long stay or traveling to remote areas.

Once in Kazakhstan, most of the usual health warnings apply. General precautions, such as washing your hands regularly and not drinking tap water unless it has been boiled, should keep harmful bacteria at bay. On the whole, be vigilant about what you eat and drink. The careful washing of fruit, even dried fruit, and vegetables is strongly recommended. Don't be tempted to sample a raisin or a slice of apple in a local fruit market, despite pressing invitations from the vendors. In rural areas, where flies are common in the warm season, be careful about eating from a *dastarkhan* (festive table) that might have been set up hours earlier. Be especially wary at intercity roadside cafés, of ready-made food at markets, and of snacks sold by vendors on trains and buses.

If possible, avoid being bitten by insects, and by blood-sucking ticks in the mountainous areas, such as those surrounding Almaty. Use a good repellent.

For emergency assistance call 103, but emergency operators, as well as medical staff, are likely to speak only Russian or Kazakh. Besides, waiting for an ambulance can take time, so it is best to go to the hospital (called *BSMP*, an acronym in Russian for Free Emergency Medical Service) by car with someone accompanying you, or by taxi. Then contact your insurance company. You can rely on local doctors for a general diagnosis, but specialist treatment or an operation is best done in your home country.

In Almaty, the medical rescue service International SOS (www.internationalsos.com) works twenty-four hours a day. Interteach (www.interteach.kz) also specializes in providing medical assistance to foreigners in English and has branches in other towns.

Apteka (in Russian) and *Darikhana* (in Kazakh) both mean "pharmacy," and there are plenty in every town and city. Most drugs can be bought without a prescription. Note that your usual brands might not be available. In Almaty the largest pharmacies are Centralnaya Apteka No. 2 (91/97 Furmanov Street) and Apteka Plus (175 Auezov Street).

SAFETY AND SECURITY

Crime is steadily on the rise, especially in the cities of Almaty and Astana, which are magnets for people from all around the country in search of work. Nevertheless, on the whole, both locals and visitors can feel safe as long as they take basic commonsense precautions. As in many big cities, foreigners can be a target for muggers at night, especially in and around popular night bars and clubs and where alcohol is consumed. Visitors should avoid walking alone at night, and keep valuables, including passports, out of sight. Avoid taking unofficial private taxis at night, unless they have been prearranged and can be trusted. If you are traveling on a train, make sure you lock your compartment door before going to sleep.

Female visitors should be aware that walking anywhere at a late hour alone, or unaccompanied by a male friend, is unwise and dangerous. Provocative clothing and heavy makeup will attract intimidating stares, and any indecent approach should be handled peacefully. If you are seriously threatened, shout for help from anybody nearby.

Many foreign travelers complain about police harassment on the street. The police have the right to check anyone's documents, and this can lead to attempts to extort cash—a practice currently being tackled by the government.

Other Risks

Almaty and other southeastern provinces north of the Tien Shan are in an active seismic zone. From time to time there are tremors in the Altai Mountains in the northeast. Levels of radiation in Kazakhstan are within international safety limits and pose no threat, even to people living in the city of Semey, close to the former Soviet nuclear testing area.

You need a permit to travel in areas along the border with China, which is a hangover from the Soviet period. This is best arranged through a local travel agent, as it can take a long time and a lot of bureaucracy to get such a permit. Travelers should also note that there have been reports of border guards firing on smugglers crossing the border illegally, and Uzbek border stations are closed from time to time without prior announcement.

chapter eight

BUSINESS BRIEFING

Until twenty years ago this was a country with a centralized economy that was part of the wider Soviet economic system. There was virtually no private sector, and no individual entrepreneurship. Capitalism, and the private ownership of assets that stands at the heart of it, were regarded as the utmost public evil. Some things haven't changed since those days, but others have. Kazakhstan is an eager learner. Foreign businessmen who first came to the country in the early 1990s will hardly recognize Kazakhstan's business environment and practices today. Seemingly without regard to the downsides of the transition, things are moving forward and moving fast.

THE BUSINESS ENVIRONMENT

Business in Kazakhstan is now largely privately owned. Most of the larger companies were formed from state companies that were privatized in the early 1990s. The majority of them operate in the extractive industries, such as oil and gas, iron and steel, copper, uranium, aluminum, or gold. These companies function under the government's close supervision, and are either funded by foreign investors or run by foreign management. Equally important are the services provided to the extractive industries, such as drilling or transport. These are divided between

foreign and local companies that, again, are predominantly former state entities. Today the state sector accounts for less than 10 percent of the economy, but the government nonetheless controls significant assets in the country's strategic oil, gas, and uranium industries, zealously protecting Kazakh interests.

Other major sectors of the economy include commerce, construction, manufacturing, agriculture, and transport. Foreign capital and expertise have a small but important share in these and other fields. In total, foreign companies account for about 5 percent of the country's businesses. Most operate by establishing a branch in the country, which is permitted to carry out full commercial activities, whereas a representative office is allowed only to undertake representative functions and to protect the interests of its head office.

Small businesses—local and foreign—concentrate on imports, real estate, construction services, and agriculture. Many local firms last for no more than three to five years, moving from one type of business to another, or giving up entrepreneurship for good.

Several factors contribute to this phenomenon: a business climate that critics say is unwelcoming to small business, frequent government interference, and underdeveloped legislation are possible reasons.

Another explanation relates to local attitudes and the general mindset (*mentalitet*, as it is often called here). As one businessman put it, "In Kazakhstan people don't think long term. Everyone wants to have immediate results and profits. Commitment, reputation, business traditions that require years of hard work—these are undervalued. Make your money as fast as you can and move on, is the prevailing attitude. You never know what may happen tomorrow."

This fear of the future derives from the instability of the early 1990s, when people could lose everything overnight. Add to this high interest rates and a culture of bribes, and the dilemma confronting the average small- or medium-scale businessman becomes understandable. One promising sign is that this sector is growing slowly, generating up to 21 percent of the country's Gross Domestic Product, and employing about 30 percent of the labor force.

As a newcomer to the local working environment you may find the general pace to be slower than in the major world centers. Also, you will find that personal relationships are of great importance: loyalty to the boss and gaining his or her good opinion, or that of close colleagues, is a much more powerful motivation than loyalty to the company. This does not mean, however, that people expect preferential treatment or a pay increase based on personal relationships. Also, an understanding of the notion "privacy" is somewhat blurred, meaning much closer social space rather than individual privacy. This, however, may not extend to include a foreigner.

The World Bank compiles a set of indicators to compare business regulation environments across economies. In 2012 Kazakhstan was ranked fifty-eighth out of 183 countries for ease of doing business. Only four years earlier it had been twenty places lower. According to the World Bank, Kazakhstan is good for starting businesses, employing workers, getting credit, paying taxes, and enforcing contracts. Exporting and importing goods is the only sector that is poorly ranked, with the many and complex procedures in place.

MANAGEMENT CULTURE

Kazakhstan's businesses typically have a strict hierarchical structure. Power is usually concentrated in the hands of a chief executive, who is the key decision maker. There is a self-explanatory popular dictum: "I am the boss, and you are a fool. If you are the boss, then I am a fool." It is uncommon for subordinates to argue with their supervisors to defend their point of view, which could lead to their dismissal. Initiatives by lower-level employees are rarely supported. Information-sharing within firms is usually limited; information and networking are more often regarded as resources for competition between colleagues.

Larger companies are dominated by Kazakh managers in their fifties and sixties who have a heavy Soviet background. Medium-sized and smaller businesses are often run by younger people of different backgrounds. Thus there is a new generation of managers in their thirties and forties who hold senior positions in private businesses, national companies, and the government. They are the first graduates of Western universities who had won scholarships from the Kazakh government or Western nations. Naturally, there are conceptual differences between this new cohort of managers and the older generation of professionals who received their education and had most of their experience during Soviet times.

Not all companies will have long-term strategies or business plans. Even fewer have a corporate Web site. If there is a Web site, it is most likely to be outdated, or unavailable in English. However, this does not always mean that a company without a strategy or a Web site is low-profile locally. There are many businesses in construction, mining, and related services whose performance is of a high standard, yet they are not accustomed to marketing their services.

LABOR RELATIONS

Labor relations are regulated by the Kazakhstan Labor Code. According to this, all employees must be given a contract that defines the terms of employment, including wage and benefits, working hours, and duties. Standard working hours are forty hours per week. The monthly wage is set by the employer but may not be less than the monthly statutory minimal wage (currently 17,439 Kazakh tenge, or around 115 US dollars).

Trade union membership—obligatory before and during Soviet times—is not common, and only the larger state-owned or formerly state-owned companies have managed to preserve their unions. Here workers have a so-called "collective agreement" with employers that protects them against dismissal. Most new businesses do not have anything like that.

The labor force accounts for about nine million people out of a total of sixteen million living in Kazakhstan. According to statistical data, every third member of those in employment has had higher education, and another third has had some sort of vocational training. The rest have at least completed secondary education. Judging from these figures, Kazakhstan has a highly skilled workforce. However, as mentioned earlier, the quality and relevance of the local education system is often criticized. In 2011 a World Bank press release highlighted "a mismatch of the demand and supply of skills." In its official report on education in Eastern Europe and Central Asia in 2012 the Bank pointed out that while Kazakhstan scored well in basic skills such as reading, writing, computation, and the ability to use technology, in the higher-order skills—communication, thinking skills, problem solving, and the ability to work independently—it was lacking.

In technical fields, such as the construction and manufacture of plant and equipment and the extractive industries, there is the even more serious problem of aging engineers and technicians. The fear is that there will simply be no one in the country with the right skills to replace them. The government, job providers, and international organizations are working together to fill the gap, but still there are virtually no experienced professionals in the technical sciences below the age of fifty.

PERSONAL RELATIONSHIPS
The human side is very important when it comes to doing business in Kazakhstan. Personal relationships matter. As we have seen, the business sector is highly

volatile, especially at the level of small businesses: companies appear and then vanish within a few years, or new owners decide to change course. The government and public sector, which are both large, mainly due to the government's heavy regulatory role, are also constantly changing. Thus, as a rule, the choice of a partner, subcontractor, or client is generally made on the basis of personal acquaintanceship with the head of the company.

Most businessmen, when meeting a prospective partner for the first time, want to know the sort of person they are going to be dealing with. To avoid possible fraud and misunderstandings in the future, it is essential to build trust. Business meals and other informal activities play an important part in making the decision to work together.

A few years ago, going to a *banya* (Russian sauna) was the most popular way for male businessmen to get to know each other and bond. What better way to open up someone's personality than by heat, vodka, and *kalyan* (hookah)! Nowadays this may seem a bit extreme, but lengthy business dinners running late with lots of eating and toasting are still a must. Business lunches are not always appropriate—they tend to be too formal and not long enough—unless they last for half the day!

BUSINESS CORRESPONDENCE

Doing business in Kazakhstan usually takes longer than in most Western countries, so a great deal of patience may be necessary. Foreign businessmen will feel this from the very first stage of establishing communication.

When setting up a meeting or negotiation it is best to target the highest management level. If you are dealing with a large company or government institution, prepare yourself for some cumbersome bureaucracy. First, send an official letter to the most senior executive, introducing your company and requesting a meeting. It should be signed by the CEO of your company and can be sent by fax. If you can arrange for your letter to be written in Russian, this will ensure that it won't sit around waiting to be translated. This doesn't mean, however, that it won't sit around somewhere else.

The response may take a long time, as the permitted period for responding to an external letter is thirty days in most big companies. If you want to speed up the process you could follow up with a phone call to the personal assistant of the addressee, or to the company's main office, but you might have to call several times, and speak to several people, before getting an answer.

Smaller companies may not require official letters. A phone call or e-mail will suffice to set up a meeting, but the introductory meeting is still important. There is a risk, however, that the addressee will not be able to understand a message written in English, or does not use e-mail as a means of communication. Thus hiring a local person who speaks Russian, English, and preferably also Kazakh would be the best way to arrange meetings and avoid the communication trap.

Be prepared for it to take more than one meeting at different levels to establish a partnership with a local firm. However, if you happen to establish a good contact with the right person, the whole process will move to the fast track. Among the "right" people are the senior management of the company concerned, highly ranked governmental officials, the company's business partners, or even family members of the company's CEO. Such a contact is best established in conversation on an informal occasion or chance encounter—for example, at a family party after an introduction by a mutual friend, or while traveling, or at a sports event.

MEETINGS

It is important to dress suitably for a meeting, depending on the type of business. Usually formal business dress is preferred, but the smaller the company the less strict the code. Successful Kazakhstani businessmen appreciate style and expensive brands, so in order to make a good impression it might be helpful to dress accordingly, but in a conservative manner.

Shaking hands is an important element of greeting, so shake hands with your Kazakh counterparts when arriving at a meeting and again when leaving. Normally, the less senior person extends a hand first to show respect. While shaking hands, eye contact is essential—lack of eye contact shows disrespect. When greeting a female business associate, wait for her to initiate the handshake. A nod with brief eye contact will usually suffice.

The exchange of business cards is common practice.

First and patronymic names are commonly used in addressing a senior person, especially if the person is of Russian origin, or you can just use Mr., Mrs., or Ms., followed by the last name. On receiving someone's card you may have to ask which is the given name and which the family name, as they do not always appear in the order you might expect. A clue is that family names often end with –ov (as in Asanov), –yev (as in Usenbayev), or –in (as in Musin) for men, and –ova, –yeva, or –ina for women. These suffixes were introduced by the Soviets to make the names sound Russian. Some Kazakh names do not have them, and may instead end with –uly (son of), –kyzy (daughter of), or –tegi. If you are not sure how to address someone, just ask.

It is helpful if your own business cards are translated into Russian on one side. If you have no bilingual cards on arrival you can have them printed in any local copy shop.

It is best to bring your own interpreter to the meeting, unless you are sure that your Kazakhstani counterpart speaks fluent English. Even if the meeting is interpreted, however, you can be sure that your counterpart will understand at least 50 percent of spoken English, so be aware of this when speaking in English with your interpreter or colleagues.

In most cases it is better to wait for your host to start the meeting and give you the floor. It may be that he, or more rarely she, will want to begin with some small talk, but during first meetings it is usually straight down to business. The code of behavior at the meeting will depend on those present: it may be formal if you are meeting senior government officials, or spontaneous if meeting business representatives. During formal meetings there is usually firm protocol and an allocated time for speaking, so when you are prompted it is best to use your time to its fullest. It is likely that you will not be given a second chance to speak.

Be prepared for expressions of criticism and doubt, which may not be directly addressed to you but to foreigners in general. It is important that you don't take this personally. If you feel you need to stand up for your point of view, it is better to address your arguments to the less senior staff—if they are present. In any case, never contradict or interrupt the main host or someone who is in a senior position to yours.

If any agreements are achieved by the end of the meeting, make sure you take note of the person in the host organization who will be responsible for their implementation. If the host invites you to a traditional Kazakh meal or to dine out, do accept the invitation, as this will consolidate further cooperation.

Smoking is prohibited in public places, but in male-dominated companies and gatherings people may smoke, even during a meeting.

PRESENTATIONS

The majority of senior Kazakh businessmen are not accustomed to doing business pitches, since most received their education in Soviet times. As anywhere else, the style of presentation will depend on the audience and the type of business. Older audiences prefer simple visual presentations with straightforward messages written in a large, clear font. It is important to remember to translate slides into Russian, even if the presentation is made in English. It is also advisable to print out a few copies of

presentations in color
(one page per slide) for
senior management.
Glossy presentations will
go down well with a younger
audience and with people in
advertising, marketing, or design,
for example, where visual presentation plays
a key role.

A time span for a presentation will usually be
discussed and set in advance. In a meeting with
several presentations, time may be limited to ten or
twenty minutes for each presenter. The timing may
be extended to thirty or forty minutes at a meeting
where you are the only presenter.

It is rare for a presenter to be interrupted, but
there will normally be time for questions after
presentations. In general, questions are a sign of
interest and attention. A lack of questions might
mean a lack of understanding or interest, but this
will not necessarily be the case.

NEGOTIATIONS
Be prepared for several rounds of negotiations
before an outcome is achieved. Again, targeting the
highest level of management is likely to be more
productive, and decisions may be made on the spot.
Negotiations with mid-level management will need
more time before the final decision is made. Be
confident but not aggressive, polite but not passive,
and flexible but not weak. Demonstrating your
expertise, and even showing off a little, may help you
to get the contract, but, as anywhere else, negotiating
styles differ depending on the circumstances.

If you asked local businessmen what sort of negotiation they see as ideal, they would tell you that it would be an open and confidential conversation, with direct and honest responses and no lies on either side. That is why the building of trustworthy relationships based on personal qualities is vital. Only then will Kazakhstani businessmen want to hear from their foreign counterparts that the product, technology, or service they are buying (and this is what most negotiations in Kazakhstan are about) is of good and reliable quality and that the company's reputation—at home or worldwide—is spotless. Many foreign businessmen are surprised to find out that the cost efficiency of their product or service is not of first importance in Kazakhstan.

Some degree of bargaining (around 10 or even up to 20 percent of the cost) is normal practice in negotiations. Once the deal is brokered there should be no further return to the subject of price.

CONTRACTS
When doing business in Kazakhstan it is vital to have a signed contract. Although the Civil Code of Kazakhstan, which regulates contracts, acknowledges written correspondence and exchange of e-mails as a formalization of agreement, only a signed contract will ensure its enforcement. Although some businesses will accept scanned copies of signatures

on contracts, it is always preferable for the contract to bear the original signatures and stamps of all the contracting parties.

Contracts are usually strictly observed. According to the *Doing Business Report 2012*, Kazakhstan ranked twenty-seventh out of 183 countries on the enforcement of contracts.

MANAGING DISAGREEMENTS

A contract must specify the governing law for resolving disagreements between parties when one of the parties is a foreign entity. Local businessmen would certainly suggest local courts as an option but do not usually insist on it.

If something goes wrong on a personal level, it is better to start trying to resolve it through a frank and confidential discussion. If the matter is raised via written correspondence it is advisable to follow it up with a face-to-face meeting, or at least over the phone. This is the fastest way to resolve most disagreements.

When problems arise in the workplace between colleagues or between management and members of staff, approaching the aggrieved colleague directly— in private—is favored. Local people are rather direct when dealing with stressful situations and can get emotional. Raising disagreements publicly might cause a scene and damage reputations on both sides.

WOMEN IN BUSINESS

By law, women in Kazakhstan are given equal opportunities in business and politics. However, in reality, the phenomenon of the "glass ceiling" is still present, reflecting the country's past as a strictly patriarchal society. In large corporations top management is mostly comprised of men, with women occupying mid-level positions. Still, almost every top management team will have at least one woman on the board, most probably responsible for accounting, budget planning, or legal affairs. In a few cases women are leading large corporations, as in Kazcommertsbank and Halyk Bank.

There are more businesswomen in small and medium enterprises, mainly in trade and the service sector. During the hard times of transition in the 1990s, just after the collapse of the Soviet economy, women demonstrated greater resilience to the stress. They often took on the role of breadwinner by moving from low-paid or no-paid teaching, engineering, or social-sector jobs to the retail or "buy and sell" sector, which had not been highly respected in Soviet times. Currently, the most successful businesswomen started out by importing clothing from China, Turkey, and later from Europe as so-called *chelnoki*, or traders. There is also a trend for the wives and daughters of men in power to open their own businesses, such as boutiques or restaurants.

The same rules apply to businesswomen as to men in Kazakhstan. If the meeting is led by a female executive, one should be careful with personal remarks, as in any society, but a brief, courteous comment on her business qualities or even her personal appearance may be well received. A greeting card or bunch of flowers sent by a courier the day before March 8, International Women's Day, would be a good gesture of respect and partnership.

CORRUPTION

In a society where position and power are almost cults and kinship ties are piously maintained, corruption is almost inevitable. The country's economy is still in a transitional stage, and has a long way to go to create a perfect business environment operated by clear legislation, an impartial judiciary, and a transparent government. The Corruption Perception Index (CPI), compiled annually by Transparency International, measures perceptions of corruption by businesspeople  and independent experts. Kazakhstan's current (2012) rating is not impressive: the country scores 2.7 out of the maximum of 10, with a ranking of 120 out of a total of 182.

The most badly affected areas are those of the judiciary, licensing and permits, customs, public procurement, and environment regulation. The good news is that the situation is improving year by year. Kazakhstan has ratified the UN Convention Against Corruption, has passed a number of laws to create a strong legislative base to fight corruption, is steadily introducing new technology into the public service sector, and is continually increasing the salaries of its civil servants. There is a separate agency for fighting economic and corruption crimes (the financial police) and an Ombudsman's Office that, at least in theory, is free from any political interference. In practice, however, this may not always be the case, and both bodies face strong criticism from the business sector and the general public.

Progress is being made, and everyone understands that corruption is a two-way street: if no one gives bribes, no one takes bribes—and vice versa. The country will eliminate corruption only when its people can hold the government accountable. In Kazakhstan, however, history has been such that it has always been the government that has held the people to account, and not the other way around.

BUSINESS GIFTS

New Year gifts between close business partners are a must, ahead of the celebrations. Cards may suffice if the relationship is important but not close enough for the exchange of gifts. Gifts are valued if they are expensive and practical. Designer ties, expensive perfume, and vintage pens are popular. Colleagues may exchange symbolic presents, such as souvenirs or sweets.

The other big occasion is March 8, International Women's Day. Every woman around you will expect at least a smile and warm congratulations. Female managers are usually snowed under with flowers and presents, and no gift will be perceived as too much or too little. Men are expected to chip in for flowers and gifts to all their female colleagues in the office.

If you know your colleague well enough, or if you have an established business partner with whom you've built a personal relationship, it is in the local culture to buy him or her a gift on his or her birthday. Again, women are often given flowers or perfume. Men usually get ties, pens, notebooks, or something similar. Colleagues in the office may buy a collective present, and anyone celebrating his or her birthday brings cakes or sweets to share, and often treats colleagues to a full lunch or dinner. There is also a tradition of celebrating anniversaries with a *toi* on a grand scale, with a guest list running to well over a hundred. It is common to invite business partners to such events, and guests usually give money (in envelopes) instead of presents. If you are invited to one of these occasions, it would be suitable to give between 100 and 500 US dollars.

chapter **nine**

COMMUNICATING

Because Kazakhstan is a mixture of cultures, you will find yourself constantly having to make adjustments when you are building your contacts and networking. The basic requirement, however, is to know one of the local languages. And you won't get very far in communicating with either Russian or Kazakh people unless you have at least elementary Russian in your arsenal.

LANGUAGE

Kazakhstan is a bilingual country. Russian is dominant in the larger cities such as Almaty and Astana and in the country's northern parts, while Kazakh is prevalent in the southern and western regions and in rural areas throughout the country. Both languages are written in the Cyrillic alphabet, so you will need to learn this to be able to read signposts and shop names. Unless you are on a guided tour, you will need to know Russian to get around the country. It is Kazakhstan's *lingua franca*.

Don't assume that anyone in Kazakhstan will speak or understand English. There is very little chance of that anywhere in the country. You won't

see any signboards, menus, labels, information in
museums and galleries, instructions on medicine
packets, contracts, or documents written in English.
So if you don't speak Russian, you'll need help. Some
visitors go to local university cafés to find a student of
English who may be willing to volunteer his or her
services.

BODY LANGUAGE

As we have seen in earlier chapters, a first-time
visitor must be prepared for a different notion of
personal space in Kazakhstan, as in much of the
former Soviet Union. This mainly applies to standing
in line. Brushing up against each other, pushing, and
even giving a light punch is common behavior in
long lines and on public transportation. When using
an ATM machine, don't be surprised if the person
behind you stands close enough to you to be able to
see your PIN and bank balance. Passersby may knock
against you without a word. If, however, someone

grabs your hand or puts an arm around you, this is a recogized gesture of apology.

In conversation, Kazakhstanis usually stand about an arm's length apart. Sometimes they are closer— just a few inches—and may even be holding the hand or whispering into the ear of their companion. When an intimate subject is raised it is common to hold the companion's elbow.

While most Kazakhstanis are physically demonstrative, better-educated people generally gesticulate less. Most of the following gestures came into the country with Russian culture.

SOME COMMON GESTURES

- Touching one's ear. A lie. This is a nonverbal expression of a Russian saying, which translates literally as "hanging pasta on one's ears."
- Flicking one's neck (vulgar). This is telling you that someone is drinking, or drunk. It may also be an invitation to have a drink.
- Crossing the arms over one's chest. Finish, stop.
- Touching wood three times, touching one's head instead of wood, or spitting three times. These are done to avoid the evil eye; similar to "knocking on wood" or "touching wood" in Western cultures.
- A finger to one's temple (vulgar). This indicates "a fool" or "nonsense."

There are impolite gestures of Russian origin that should be avoided, such as pointing your finger at a person, sticking your tongue out, or putting your thumb between your index and third finger, which is a childish or impolite expression meaning "Don't even think about it."

The Western "OK" sign (connecting the thumb with one's index finger) is not widely used, but is understood. The victory sign (holding up one's index and third finger) is generally understood as "two" rather than "victory."

Gestures specific to Kazakh culture include putting a hand on the empty cup after drinking tea, which indicates that no more is wanted. After a meal, stroking one's face with both hands (as after Muslim prayers) is thanking Allah for the food, but is also a signal that the person is about to leave. A respectful person avoids walking closely past an older person, as this is regarded as rude.

Smiles and Greetings

A smile is not considered to be necessary to politeness in Kazakhstan. It has a more intimate meaning, and is reserved for close friends and acquaintances. You won't see smiling faces around you when you are out and about, or even when you meet a business partner for the first time, but this doesn't mean you are not welcome. The better you know a person, the wider the smile will be.

There are clear rules about greetings between men in Kazakh culture. Men greet each other (and often say farewell) with a firm handshake. A younger person extends both hands with the palms up, and the older person holds and shakes both hands. In some parts of Kazakhstan the younger person may first put his right hand over his heart and bow slightly. A handshake followed by an embrace is common between friends and business partners. They shake right hands first and then embrace.

Kazakh men don't usually kiss each other on meeting, but Russian men do.

Women don't normally shake hands, except in a business environment. In strictly traditional families, Kazakh women and especially daughters-in-law greet their in-laws with a bow.

FORMS OF ADDRESS

Addressing a young person is very simple: use first names. In Kazakh it is also common to address a person younger than yourself as "sister" (*karyndas*), "brother" (*baurym*), or even "daughter" (*kyzym*) or "son" (*balam*). Senior people on the street and at home alike are addressed simply as "aunt" (*tate, apa*) or "uncle" (*aga*). In a friendly situation, adult Kazakh men of a similar age address each other by diminutives of first names. Russian men may also greet Kazakh friends in this way.

The formal way to address a senior Russian or Kazakh is to use the name and patronymic (the father's name plus the suffix –ovna or –yevna for a female and –ovych or –yevich for a male). When addressing middle-aged Kazakhs, this purely Russian form of address may not be appropriate. If you are addressing an English speaker, you can use Mr. or Ms. To address a stranger, use the Russian forms of "young woman" (*devushka*), "young man" (*paren*), "woman" (*jenshina*), "man" (*mujchina*), "boy" (*malchik*), or "girl" (*devochka*).

HUMOR

Historically, Kazakhs had a rich verbal culture, and jokes were part of it. Kazakh humor today can range from sophisticated satire to teasing, telling jokes, and simply having a good laugh. Centuries ago the best jokes mocked ignorant fools, both rich and poor, and it is not dissimilar today. Legendary folk characters such as Aldar Kose and Hodja (Molla) Nasreddin, who are famous all across Central Asia, remain popular alongside present-day characters such as the traffic police officer Tengebay (*tenge* means money, and *bay* means lord), from the TV comedy show *Nasha Kzasha*, and the omnipresent Soviet-era Kazakh who is hilariously boastful, ridiculously ambitious, and yet a character you can't help loving. The latter may sound like the English comedian Sacha Baron Cohen's infamous creation Borat Sagdiyev, but Borat is the most hated comic character in Kazakhstan, for obvious reasons. The Kazakh Everyman is more like the one in the following old Soviet-era joke that still goes around.

The Kazakh Everyman

Three men—an American, a Russian, and a Kazakh—returned from a space mission on the Moon. "What was the aim of your mission?" a journalist asked. "To see whether we can build a space station there," said the American. "To see whether we can propagate Communist ideas," answered the Russian. "What about you?" the journalist asked the Kazakh, who looked as if he were the most important member of the crew. "Oh," said the Kazakh, appearing suddenly humble and embarrassed, "I was sure I'd meet a relative of mine up there".

Strictly speaking, Kazakhstani humor serves two different audiences—Kazakh speakers and Russian speakers. *Tamasha* is the most popular comic sketch show in Kazakh, followed keenly by families all across the country. The humor is simple and straightforward, with lots of parody, but is not without its charm, tackling, at times, the most acute issues of everyday life. *Baurzhan Show* is another Kazakh favorite, a creation of the former *Tamasha* star Baurzhan Ibragimov, who established his own comedy theater in the early 1990s. From more recent TV shows there is a comic sketch called *Azil-Studio*, which features a light and humorous take on everyday situations.

Kazakhstani-made TV programs in Russian have the daunting task of rivaling Russian shows that are very popular with local audiences, and very few succeed. The best-known local TV program, *Nasha Kzasha* (a Kazakh version of the British parody show *Little Britain*), in its early seasons was an exception that conquered viewers' hearts and minds with its hilarious sketches on local culture and norms.

THE MEDIA
TV and Radio

There is a mix of private and state-owned TV and radio companies. At the nationwide level there are eleven TV and five radio stations. Forty more TV channels and more than thirty-five radio stations broadcast at the local level. There are also a number of cable TV channels.

TV is the nation's main source of news and its favorite media form, with "made in Russia" content most popular with the masses. Turkish and South Korean soap operas bring big viewing figures to local stations. Programs made in Kazakhstan and in the Kazakh language are gradually gaining favor, supported by government funding. Current affairs and political programs rarely demonstrate exemplary journalism, due to tight state control, self-censorship, and low ethical standards, but the entertainment side of TV has taken off.

The local music industry is in the early stages of development, and thus foreign music (European, US, and Russian) dominates airtime on the radio. The most popular radio stations in Kazakhstan are Retro FM, Radio NS, and Russkoe Radio-Eurasia. There is also the recently opened Classical FM station. The younger generation prefers stations like Energy FM, specializing in electronic music.

The Press

There are a large number of print media outlets—nearly two thousand newspapers and periodicals, around 85 percent of which are privately owned. Kazakh officials mention this every now and then as a demonstration of freedom of speech in the country, but most of the publications have dismal circulation figures and are printed on an irregular basis. Newspapers and magazines that make an impact are few, and are under constant scrutiny by the authorities, if not actually directly controlled by them. The biggest newspapers (in descending order of circulation) are *Karavan*, *Vremya*, *Liter*, *Novoe Pokolenie*, *Express K*, and *Respublika Kz*.

Internet
Delivering high-quality Internet in a country the size of Kazakhstan is a major challenge, though it is gradually becoming more generally available. The Internet has given new opportunities to those critical of the authorities and has enabled many independent newspapers to go online. However, this new form of freedom of speech was tamed a little when media legislation was amended to curtail the activity of independent bloggers.

SERVICES
Telephone
The landline telephone services in Kazakhstan are accessible, reliable, and cheap. The leading service provider is the state-owned Kazakhtelecom. In-city fixed-line calls are free to another fixed-line phone. A charge of roughly 10 tenge (7 cents) per minute is applied for intercity calls within Kazakhstan.

To make an intercity call, first dial 8, wait for the tone, and then dial the city code and the number.

To make an international call, first dial 8, then 10. International calls are more expensive, costing roughly 2 US dollars per minute, though you can also buy phone cards to make cheaper international calls.

It is almost impossible to find public telephones in Kazakhstan, so it is much easier to buy a cell phone. Cell phones have gradually become the normal means of communication. The major operators are GSM-Kazakhstan (K'Cell, Activ), KarTel (Beeline), Altel (Pathword, Dalacom), and MTS (Tele 2). Most use the GSM 900/1800 standards, though Altel uses the CDMA2000-1X standard.

Cell phone services are expensive compared to European markets. A minute of outgoing talk costs up to 22 US cents, though incoming calls are free. Another advantage of cell phone services in Kazakhstan is that you can easily buy and load your GSM phones with a "pay as you go" SIM card.

3G and GPRS connections are available, and there is free Wi-Fi in cafés and public places in Almaty and Astana. However, elsewhere both the availability and speed of Wi-Fi connections may be less satisfactory. There are plans to introduce 4G and LTE technologies in Kazakhstan by 2015. Broadband Internet is provided by many operators, including Kazakhtelecom (Megaline or IDnet), Alma TV, and Beeline.

Mail
Mail services are represented by the state KazPost and private services such as DHL and Ponyexpress. If you are sending a package to an address in Kazakhstan or abroad, DHL is a reliable though expensive option. National post is cheaper but less secure. An even cheaper, unofficial, but more reliable option is to send mail or packages to another city by train in the care of the conductors. You simply go to

the train station at the time the right train is due, choose one conductor among the many who accompany the carriages, give him written instructions along with the package, and ask the price, which is likely to be 1,000 to 3,000 tenge. Then you will need to give the recipient the details so that he or she can personally collect the package from the conductor, in his wagon, at the end of the journey.

CONCLUSION

Kazakhstan is blessed with natural resources. Its economic future looks bright and the country is open for business and receptive to foreign visitors. Most of its treasures—oil, gas, mineral resources, and archeological riches—are under the surface. The great Kazakh Steppe, which dominates the landscape, although seemingly empty, has rivers, lakes, hills, forests, and interesting wildlife. But what makes the country special is its strong, open people. They have a unique history of social and political tolerance and adaptability, are heirs to a clan-based nomadic culture that cherishes ancestry and lineage, and are immediately responsive and generous toward anyone in need of help.

We hope that *Culture Smart! Kazakhstan* will enable you to see things through Kazakh eyes, and to enjoy your visit to its fullest. Take time to meet the people halfway, and you'll soon join the ranks of appreciative travelers to this remarkable country.

Further Reading

Robbins, Christopher. *In Search of Kazakhstan. The Land that Disappeared*. London: Profile Books, 2008.

Aitken, Jonathan. *Kazakhstan and Twenty Years of Independence*. London: Continuum Publishing Corporation, 2012.

Schreibe, Dagmar, and Jeremy Tredinnick. *Kazakhstan: Nomadic Routes from Caspian to Altai*. Hong Kong: Odyssey Publications, 2012.

Olkott, Martha Brill. *The Kazakhs. Studies of Nationalities in the USSR*. Stanford, CA: Hoover Institution Press, 1987.

Dave, Bhavna. *Kazakhstan. Ethnicity, Language and Power*. Abingdon, Oxford/ New York, NY: Routledge, 2007.

Fergus, Michael, and Janar Jandosova (eds.) *Kazakhstan: Coming of Age*. London: Stacey International, 2003.

Abazov, Rafis (ed.). *Green Desert. The Life and Poetry of Olzhas Suleimenov*. San Diego, CA: Cognella, 2010.

Shayakhmetov, Mukhamet. *The Silent Steppe. The Story of a Kazakh Nomad under Stalin*. London: Stacey International, 2006.

Smith, Tracy S. *Dear Chums! I am in Kazakhstan! Bloomington*, IN: Trafford Publishing, 2012.

Stark, Sören, and Karen S. Rubinson (eds). *Nomads and Networks: The Ancient Art and Culture of Kazakhstan*. Exhibition catalogue. Princeton, NJ: Princeton University Press, 2012.

culture smart! kazakhstan

Index

Acknowledgment

I would like to thank Nick Nugent for helping me with the editing and being such a wonderful friend.